SPECTACU
HELMETS
16th–19th C

Japan Society and Kodansha International

LAR
OF JAPAN
entury

Organized by Japan House Gallery and
the Association for the Research and Preservation of Japanese Helmets and Armor

This catalogue was published on the occasion of an exhibition
organized by Japan House Gallery and the Association for the Research
and Preservation of Japanese Helmets and Armor, Tokyo.
The exhibition was shown at Japan House Gallery, New York,
and the Asian Art Museum of San Francisco in the fall of
1985 and early winter, 1986.

The exhibition and catalogue were made possible in part by the
generous support of the Chase Manhattan Bank, N.A., and the
Sumitomo Group. Additional grants awarded by the National
Endowment for the Humanities and the National Endowment for
the Arts, Washington, D.C., contributed importantly to the
exhibition program. The Japan Society presentation benefitted
from the continuing support of Lila Acheson Wallace, the
Andrew W. Mellon Foundation, and the Friends of Japan House
Gallery. The exhibition was made possible in San Francisco by a
generous contribution from the Sumitomo Group to the
Asian Art Museum of San Francisco.

Editor: Alexandra Munroe

Designed by Kiyoshi Kanai and Andrea Wollensak
Set in Century Schoolbook by U.S. Lithograph Inc., New York
Printed by Nissha Printing Co. Ltd., Kyoto, Japan
Distributed throughout the world by Kodansha International
Library of Congress Catalogue Card Number: 85-081280
ISBN 0-87011-784-X
ISBN 4-7700-1284-5 (in Japan)

All photographs courtesy of the Association for the Research and
Preservation of Japanese Helmets and Armor, Tokyo, except
where otherwise indicated.

Note: In catalogue section, height refers to dimension of the form
which comprises or surmounts the helmet bowl; it does not include
the dimension of protruding or extending decorations.

CONTENTS

FOREWORD

This exhibition, *Spectacular Helmets*, is the first in the United States devoted to the art of the Japanese helmet. The presentation, exceptional from visual, critical and scholarly points of view, contains helmets from important collections in Japan never before shown outside that country.

Indeed, this catalogue, intended for students of Japanese art as well as for the general public, is the first major publication in English on the subject, and we are grateful to the Japan Society and the Association for the Research and Preservation of Japanese Helmets and Armor, Tokyo for their scholarship and research.

It is especially noteworthy that these helmets, essentially utilitarian, were developed and embellished through the centuries so that their beauty as art objects gradually became more important than their original function. They may be appreciated by viewers interested in history, religion, sociology, philosophy, aesthetics, by those interested in military history, craft and art history, or simply in Japanese art and culture.

Chase has long been associated with Japan Society, and we are delighted to continue this partnership by making this important exhibition possible.

Willard C. Butcher
Chairman of the Board
The Chase Manhattan Bank, N.A.

We of the Sumitomo Group are pleased and proud to have a part in this magnificent presentation to the American people of the rich legacy of one of Japan's great artistic and social traditions.

The samurai warriors disappeared from Japanese life over a century ago, much like the knights of feudal Europe, who vanished with the rise of the modern nation-state. Yet, just as Western chivalry survives in song and story, so also the samurai's way of life—his spirit of selfless service and his devotion to beauty —endures in such rare creations of fine art as the *kawari kabuto*.

From my own experience of several happy years in the United States, I know the sensitive appreciation so many Americans have for Japan's artistic heritage. I am confident, therefore, that this unique exhibition will touch a wide American audience, deepening their interest and their understanding of the Japanese people and their culture.

This exhibition would not have been possible without the generous cooperation of the Association for the Research and Preservation of Japanese Helmets and Armor (Nihon Katchū Bugu Hozen Kenkyū-kai) and the Agency for Cultural Affairs of the Japanese Government (Bunka-chō). We are grateful to both these organizations, to our fellow sponsors of this exhibition, and especially to the Japan Society, for its leadership and faultless taste through the years in presenting Japan to America.

Tadashi Itoh
President, Sumitomo Corporation
on behalf of the Sumitomo Group

LENDERS

Ana Hachiman Shrine, Tokyo
Sei'ichi Asano, Tokyo
Iwao Fujimoto, Tokyo
Hajime Fujita, Okayama Prefecture
Fukuoka City Museum, Fukuoka Perfecture
Kiyotsugu Kuritomo, Hiroshima Prefecture
Saburō Makita, Tokyo
Tadamasa Mitsuhashi, Tokyo
Keisuke Nakamiya, Osaka
Tatsuo Nakamura, Kyoto
National Museum of Japanese History, Chiba Prefecture
Nishimura Museum, Yamaguchi Prefecture
Tadao Nishiyama, Saitama Prefecture
Motoyuki Shiroaya, Hyogo Prefecture
Suntory Museum of Art, Tokyo
Takatsu Kobunka Kaikan (Takatsu Traditional Culture Foundation), Kyoto
Fusao Tomoda, Kyoto
Ueda Municipal Museum, Nagano Prefecture
Uesugi Shrine, Yamagata Prefecture
Yamaguchi Kobunka Zaidan (Yamaguchi Traditional Culture Foundation), Tokyo
Takuji Yokota, Hiroshima Prefecture
Shizue Yonetani, Kyoto
Yoshiaki Yoshida, Saitama Prefecture
Tadao Yoshii, Osaka

ACKNOWLEDGEMENTS

The Association for the Preservation and Research of Japanese Helmets and Armor, co-sponsor and organizer of the exhibition with Japan House Gallery in association with the Asian Art Museum of San Francisco, is an institution dedicated to an important and ancient art form. Mr. Munenori Akagi, distinguished chairman of the Association (known in Japan as the Nihon Katchū Bugu Kenkyū Hozonkai), has worked ceaselessly over the last years to advance this exhibition. He has contributed importantly to our knowledge of objects and collections in Japan, and he has guided us throughout the development of this project. We are most grateful for Mr. Akagi's leadership.

Spectacular Helmets of Japan is the result of several years of negotiation, organization, and research involving many individuals and institutions here and in Japan. We are very pleased to have been able to work again with the Agency for Cultural Affairs, Tokyo. Our way has been made smoother in Japan by the Agency's generous assistance. We are grateful to the commissioner, Mr. Shumon Miura; the director of the Fine Arts Division, Mr. Nobuyoshi Yamamoto; and to Inspector Dr. Yūichi Hiroi, a noted authority in the field of metalwork and an important contributor to this exhibition and catalogue.

The *kawari kabuto*, literally extraordinary or spectacular helmets which are the subject of this exhibition, are rare, old, and fragile. For these reasons, the itinerary for the exhibition was necessarily limited in the United States to one other institution. We are fortunate here in being able to work with the Asian Art Museum of San Francisco, an institution renowned for its collections. Our planning was made easy by the good work of former director, Rene-Yvon Lefebvre d'Argence; senior curator and acting director, Clarence F. Shangraw; curator of Japanese Art, Yoshiko Kakudo; and as well by the members of the Asian Art Commission's Committee on Acquisitions, Loans, and Exhibitions.

Dr. John Whitney Hall, Whitney Griswold Professor Emeritus of History and former chairman of the Department of History at Yale University, and author and distinguished authority on Japan, provided us with much valuable insight into the history of Japan in the late sixteenth and early seventeenth centuries. His essay enriches this book with a portrait of the daimyo of this period. Professor Hall is a former member of the board of directors of Japan Society, and we especially welcome his renewed association with us.

Isamu Noguchi is an artist whose work uniquely spans the globe. It is a great honor that he has graciously agreed to write for these pages, sharing his splendid perspective on Japan's small sculptures.

Mr. Richard Gage, an outstanding translator living in Japan, kindly consented to undertake the difficult task of rendering into English and adapting for an American readership the scholarly texts for the catalogue. His ability to combine patience, with us—and speed, with the manuscript, defies description, but may we simply note a special thanks for his superior work. Alexandra Munroe, editor for Japan House Gallery, worked closely with the authors and curators in the preparation and research of the catalogue. Kiyoshi Kanai produced the design of this catalogue, and we are grateful to him and to his assistant Andrea Wollensak for their continuing contribution to our exhibition and publication program. Maryell Semal, assistant director of Japan House Gallery, worked determinedly on the logistics and installation of the exhibition. Her arrangements were, as usual, flawless. Cleo Nichols produced the brilliant setting in New York for the helmets, and Mitsuko Maekawa, the Gallery's research assistant, provided us with much of the primary research upon which the exhibition was built. At Japan Society, Claire Bettag, director of development, is owed a special thanks for her extraordinary assistance in making this exhibition possible, and to director of publications, Sandra Faux, we are grateful for her coaching of the catalogue's production. Intern Amy Cardamone assisted invaluably in the preparation of the bibliography and chronology.

We are always pleased to join the great corporations of America and Japan in presenting a major exhibition of Japanese art in the United States. Japan Society is honored on this occasion with the participation of the Chase Manhattan Bank, N.A. and the Sumitomo Group. We are grateful for the generous support each has given to the exhibition and catalogue, *Spectacular Helmets of Japan.*

Grants awarded by the National Endowment for the Humanities and the National Endowment for the Arts of Washington, D.C. contributed importantly to the realization of this program, and we acknowledge here our gratitude for this federal support. We are grateful too for the continuing support of Lila Acheson Wallace, The Andrew W. Mellon Foundation, and the Friends of Japan House Gallery.

For guidance of the Gallery's programs, thanks are always due to Lily Auchincloss, chairman of the Friends, Porter McCray, chairman of the Arts Advisory Committee, and to David MacEachron, president of Japan Society. We are blessed with their good leadership.

Rand Castile
Director
Japan House Gallery

The Asian Art Museum of San Francisco is pleased to participate with Japan Society and the Association for the Research and Preservation of Japanese Helmets and Armor in this unprecedented opportunity to display an art form never previously shown in an American museum. There is no doubt that this first major showing of *Spectacular Helmets of Japan: 16th-19th Century* and the publication of its catalogue will bring the creative genius of unknown Japanese craftsmen to a new public awareness and knowledge. Through this greater appreciation, it is hoped that we can be lead to greater international understanding.

This is our initial joint venture with Japan House Gallery, and we are honored to be the only other American institution involved in this unique sharing of Japanese treasures drawn from important private and public collections throughout that country.

For their support of the San Francisco showing, we are particularly grateful to the executives of the Sumitomo Group, whose major funding made San Francisco's ardent interest in the exhibition a reality for this museum. We also thank The Honorable Masaki Seo, Consul General of Japan in San Francisco, for his personal interest and support. We are grateful as well to Mayor Dianne Feinstein and the San Francisco Board of Supervisors for their annual fiscal support of our exhibition programs.

We wish to extend personal thanks to Mr. Rand Castile, director of Japan House Gallery, and to Mr. Munenori Akagi, distinguished chairman of the Association for the Research and Preservation of Japanese Helmets and Armor; to Yoshiko Kakudo, our curator of Japanese art; and to the Asian Art Commission's Committee on Acquisitions, Loans and Exhibitions, all of whom played major, persuasive roles in bringing the exhibition to us and so enriching our cultural lives.

Clarence F. Shangraw
Acting Director
Asian Art Museum of San Francisco

NO DIVISION BETWEEN ARTIST AND MASK

Isamu Noguchi

Kawari Kabuto, the Japanese warrior's helmet, has more use than to protect the head. More mask than hat, it is a disguise to transform the wearer into a personage of otherworldly ferocity. Intended to frighten the enemy, an even more subtle function may be to transform the wearer. Thus garbed, his true status confirmed, he is the samurai dedicated to death governed by a code beyond the pale and beyond reproach. The mask of terror becomes the man himself.

The role of art in this change of personality is through sculpture. Some *kabuto* we recognize as great works of art. In these, the artist himself identifies as one with his creation. There is no division between artist and mask any more than there is in nature, where the beetle devises his own attire to assure survival. Art is the means.

When I was ten my mother kept me out of school and sought to teach me herself —botany and the like. She had me apprenticed to the local carpenter in Chigasaki. At one point, I became involved with making hats; that is, hierarchic affairs such as that winged one of Perseus giving invisibility to slay the Medusa, protected from being turned to stone. This gives me my only right to comment on *kabuto*. With a residue of experience beyond that of other children who make a helmet of origami and are soon off to war.

The hats I made were my first expression as an artist, invisible and invincible as Perseus, in the only period of my education that now makes sense.

With the viewing of great *kabuto* we are privileged to recognize the artist, now himself the warrior, or should I say, as all of us—we are made to see that we are ourselves the warrior doomed to die.

It may be said that all effigy-making offers a similar transcendence of identity. We identify with the football player because of his costume. Star Wars are presented as our last noble adventure—again imaged in medieval attire—from which there will be no return. The difference with *kabuto* is where the individual artist comes in—inward changing—more like the mud-caked savage than with concerns for public recognition—and the wearer too, to the extent of his own true trance and devotion.

The Summer Attack on Osaka Castle, 1615. (Detail of six-panel screen painting, 17th century. Osaka Castle. Photo © Sekai Bunka Photo.)

ON HELMETS

Rand Castile

Helmets are crowns to warriors, and for those who grew up with epics, the names of helmets are incantatory: The Norman casque, the basinet, the sallet, and tilting heaume, the armet, and the morion. These still stir the boy warrior. And the fancy burgonet, so typically French, with cheekpiece and aspiring ornament, the high-crested Spanish cabasset, and Shakespeare's beaver, in *Henry IV*:

> All furnished, all in Arms;
> All plumed like Estridges that with the wind
> Baited like Eagles having lately bathed,
> Glittering in golden coats like images
> As full of spirit as the month of May,
> And gorgeous as the sun at Midsummer:
> Wanton as youthful goats, wild as young bulls,
> *I* saw young Harry with his Beaver on,
> His cushes on his thighs, gallant armed,
> Rise from the ground like feathered Mercury,
> And vaulted with such ease into his seat,
> As if an angel dropped down from the clouds,
> To turn and wind a fiery Pegasus,
> And witch the world with noble horsemanship.
>
> [Act IV, sc. 1]

For the champion, the helmet bounds the brow like a victorious wreath. It is the very symbol of his triumph and dignity. For the fallen, *his* helmet and sword are the spoils first lost.

For most Westerners, Japanese helmets were encountered at the movies. But who could forget the effect of helmets in the work of Akira Kurosawa. In *Throne of Blood*, Toshiro Mifune rides with Minoru Chiaki into the fog and out, horses wet, the long bow gleaming, banners stiff at the back! The helmets they wear are powerful. Mifune's is fronted with a crescent moon. His companion's has two mounted prongs, the *kuwagata* form.

The highly-designed helmets known as *kawari kabuto*, which are the subject of this exhibition, were influenced by the forms and decorations introduced by the Portuguese, Spanish, and Dutch emissaries in the mid-sixteenth century. The contemporary Spanish cabasset, high with the flights of decorative invention, must have struck the Japanese as dramatic and more impressive than their own traditional designs. Surely they took these as models and transmogrified them into something spectacularly Japanese.

Following the bitter, relentless, and ruinous wars for unification, the dread conflicts of the sixteenth and early seventeenth centuries, Japan emerged from smoke and ashes into a period of relative but long-lived peace. Sumptuary laws of the new Edo shogunate subsequently froze in place styles of dress and placed strict limitations upon the population. Armor, too, was restricted according to rank. These provisions had the effect of stultifying the design of helmets. There was little to be done for the imaginative lord who might have wished to change the form or decoration of his traditional headgear.

The individuality expressed in the *kawari kabuto* was a product of a unique time in Japanese history, a kind of "hundred flowers blooming," but with established unification and the subjugation of all lords and samurai to a central authority in the seventeenth century, the blaze of individualism dimmed inexorably among Japan's ruling military aristocracy. The nation turned inward, criticism was closed, forms were replicated; there was little cause for invention. As there were no battles to be fought, such helmets as there were were meant to signify one's political and social position. The helmets were worn by high-ranking soldiers and lords in procession and for receptions of state.

The late twentieth century has seen a revival of interest in the helmet. This probably has more to do with the success of Honda, Suzuki, and Kawasaki motorbikes and -cycles than of anything else, save Darth Vader and the Kurosawa creations. The new Japanese speedskater helmets are elegant, streamlined, and colorful. (One of them is now in the collection of the Museum of Modern Art, New York.) The field has come full-circle. The recent helmets are, after all, for protection.

A PERSONAL IMAGE OF POWER:
THE RISE OF THE DAIMYO WARLORD

John Whitney Hall

Japanese history does not record many periods when uninhibited individualism was encouraged or even tolerated. The sixteenth century, however, was just such a period. It was a time when in almost every sphere of life, in political and social organization, economic capacity, climate of thought, and artistic expression, major changes took place across the land.

The first half of the sixteenth century was the darkest part of Japan's Sengoku era (1477–1573), the period of "the country at war." Following the outbreak of the Ōnin War (1467–77), which ravaged the capital city of Kyoto, the country was torn apart into small, nearly autonomous territories whose overlords warred with each other for local advantage. Central authority was ignored with impunity. The emperor and his court retained little more than a ceremonial presence, while the head of the Ashikaga house—shogun and chief of the warrior estate—had been reduced to political impotence by his own vassals.

From roughly the middle of the sixteenth century, however, the drift toward chaotic fragmentation began to slow, and a process of consolidation set in. By 1600, the foundation had been laid for a new central authority, the Edo shogunate, that was to keep the peace for the following two and a half centuries. The driving force behind this development was, in broadest terms, the warrior aristocracy —the *bushi* or samurai estate—now organized into effective military and administrative units under the command of local military lords, or daimyo. As the process of military consolidation progressed, the daimyo converted their domains into ever-more concentrated military organizations, building imposing residential castles and drawing around them large standing bodies of samurai fighters. Whereas in earlier days the lower levels of the samurai had lived in the countryside serving both as land managers and fighters in reserve, they now were drawn off the land into the daimyo's castle towns. A clear line was drawn between the samurai and the peasants who remained in the villages. At long last the samurai had become by legal definition and style of life a ruling warrior aristocracy, alone permitted to bear the surname and wear the long sword, *katana*.

There is a special poignancy in the fact that much of the period of consolidation in Japan was observed by visitors from Europe. Jesuit priests, Portuguese and Dutch traders were given easy access to the Japanese islands from the mid-sixteenth century, and their reports offer vivid glimpses of this fast-moving age. Contact with Europe had tangible impact on Japan's domestic affairs, specifically with the introduction of firearms in 1543. Unquestionably hastening the unification process, the musket and cannon changed the requirements for castle construction, and influenced as well the style of individual combat, touching the technology of armor and inspiring new designs for the warrior helmet.

We tend to think of the sixteenth century in Japan as a time of destructive civil warfare and ruthless attacks against religious orders, both Buddhist and Christian. But in terms of statecraft, the country made enormous strides. The command techniques perfected by the larger military lords made possible a mobilization of civil and military manpower on an unprecedented scale. The sheer growth in national power—the capacity, for example, to assemble, equip, and feed armies numbering into the hundreds of thousands—was astounding for the time and place. (The ability not only to mobilize but to deliver armed forces at will over great distances is dramatically illustrated in Toyotomi Hideyoshi's 1592 invasion of Korea. Having successfully united all daimyo under his command in

1590, Hideyoshi required only two years to assemble a force of 160,000 men that successfully overran the Korean peninsula, though without a lasting occupation.)

The most prominent public symbol of the age of military consolidation was without question the multi-storied castle, or *tenshu-kaku*, that stood at the center of each lord's domain. The Jesuit missionary Luis Frois was among many Europeans who expressed astonishment at the size and impregnability of the Japanese military establishments. In particular he admired the *tenshu-kaku* that were "far more noble and splendid in appearance" than those in the West.

Of the many artifacts that make up the more personal image we have of the military elite of sixteenth-century Japan, the one that best exemplifies the traditional samurai spirit is surely the long sword, or *katana*. From early times, the sword was the chosen weapon of the warrior, admired, even worshiped, by those who were privileged to live by its seeming supernatural powers. Thus, although the samurai adopted the gun for the business of military conquest, once the fighting was over, he returned to the sword. A sacred imperial regalia, along with the mirror and jewel, the sword remains today that part of samurai weaponry most dear to the Japanese.

But the artifact that speaks most eloquently of the spirit of the age of consolidation must be the fantastic helmets, or *kawari kabuto*, designed for the military leaders of that tumultuous chapter in Japanese history. There is something bizarre and eccentric about the helmets that distinguish them from the sword as

Portrait of Toyotomi Hideyoshi in the year of his death, 1598. Born of less than samurai status, Hideyoshi rose to power by winning military victory after victory in Japan's struggle for unification in the late sixteenth century. As parvenu warlord, he took every opportunity to enhance his image with extravagant displays of wealth, rank, and style. He is depicted here in the costume of a high ranking court noble. (Detail of hanging scroll painting, 16th century. Photo © Sekai Bunka Photo.)

17

personal expressions of the user. But, unlike the *katana* whose history of manufacture spans well beyond a millenium, the heyday of the creative impulse that produced the *kawari kabuto* was relatively short. Confined to the last stages of the work of unification, their design reached its peak during the last decades of the sixteenth century and the first three of the seventeenth. But once the fighting was over and a stable peace assured, the country turned in upon itself. In all walks of life, regulations were imposed on the freedom of private expression. Castle construction was frozen in place. Most remarkable of all, the whole technology of firearms that had won the peace was put aside. In a like manner, the fantastic helmets, though still admired, were definitely out of phase with the mood of the "Great Peace," and little effort was made to experiment with new and bolder designs, although as this exhibition demonstrates, such helmets continued to be made for ceremonial occasions. The *kawari kabuto* spoke to a single moment in Japanese history, and their appearance as well as their disappearance must be understood in the context of the long evolution of the military aristocracy as a separate estate in Japan. It is a story that stretches from the dawn of Japanese history into our own times.

The earliest evidence we have of the existence of a military elite in Japan is drawn from the large burial mounds dating from the fourth through seventh centuries A.D. Among the funeral objects associated with these tombs are clay figures, or *haniwa*, showing men wearing armor apparently ancestral to the historic style of helmet and body armor in Japan. Separate finds of single-bladed long swords, horse trappings and other military equipment suggest the presence of a class of mounted warriors who possessed the coersive power to command the construction of these large mounds. The critical questions, for which we have no certain answers, are whether the ruling elite of this time was divided into civil and military branches, and whether the conduct of military affairs was a separate skill cultivated as a professional activity on a hereditary basis.

In the seventh and eighth centuries, the elite families of the area surrounding the capital at Nara were mainly a civil nobility. For roughly two centuries, they systematically modeled their political institutions on those of imperial China. Armed forces were organized in the continental fashion, using manpower drawn from the cultivator class under the command of officers dispatched by the central government. Within the aristocracy, there was evidently a military command service whose ranks were filled by and large with men from the provinces.

But the conscript system did not long survive, and instead the central government began to rely on men drawn from what we might call a provincial gentry class. By the tenth century, a growing number of provincial families had begun to take up the bearing of arms as a profession in addition to their functions as provincial or district officials. Here clearly were the ancestors of the historic samurai. They were as yet not conscious of being a separate class. Rather, they stayed within the provincial administration as junior officers, serving the court as vice-governors, district chiefs, constables, and managers of private estates.

During the last half of the twelfth century, families of this type gained a sense of separate identity as a military elite through their involvement in several military operations. Leadership in the provinces, both political and military, was provided by a group of middle-ranking aristocratic families, like the Minamoto and

Haniwa of warrior. Clay figures found in the burial mounds of the Kofun period (300-552 B.C.) are the earliest evidence of the existence of a military elite in Japan. (6th century, Tokyo National Museum. Photo courtesy of the Bunka-chō).

The Tale of the Heike. These scenes from the epic tale of the twelfth-century struggle between the Heike and Genji clans illustrate early styles of samurai combat and armor. Although an Edo-period interpretation, this narrative work faithfully depicts the traditional yoroi *cuirass,* kuwagata *helmets, and* eboshi *hats worn by warriors of the late Heian and Kamakura periods. (Detail of six-fold screen painting, 18th century. Asian Art Museum of San Francisco. Photo courtesy of the Collection.)*

Taira, distant offshoots of the imperial house. Competition among these groups led increasingly to open warfare. The most widespread and turbulent of these, the Gempei War (1182–85), was fought out across the Japanese islands as military houses turned on each other in a contest for office and land. The task of bringing the military houses under control was led by Minamoto Yoritomo (1147–99), founder of Japan's first military government. Heir to the headship of the prestigious Minamoto house, he rallied to his support large numbers of provincial military families, forming a military power center in Kamakura, three hundred miles east of Kyoto. His status as military chief of the country was recognized by his inclusion into the high court nobility as Commander of the Right Imperial Guard. Added to this was his appointment in 1192 as Sei-i-tai-shōgun, generally referred to simply as shogun, a title that was eventually interpreted to signify that its bearer possessed the authority to command the military estate as a whole. But as later developments were to prove, Yoritomo's most significant achievement was his acquisition of the authority to install the posts of military land steward (*jitō*) and military governor (*shugo*) in all provinces. Through these offices, he and his successors eventually gained the right to intervene in the fiscal and judicial affairs of all landed proprietorships, state and private, in Japan.

It is commonly assumed that the political system created by Yoritomo was the first step in the development of a feudal order. This is based on the mistaken belief that all appointments as military land stewards and military governors were bound to Yoritomo as his private housemen, or *gokenin*. We now know that the number of housemen was relatively small. The country remained divided administratively into provinces and districts, and members of the military families still functioned as officials of the provincial administration under institutions that were subordinate to civil officials at the court in Kyoto. Yet there was no denying that Kamakura represented a rival center of power.

The outstanding achievement of the Kamakura era was the promulgation in 1232 of the *Goseibai shikimoku*, a legal code that defined the role of the warrior in a polity that had long been confined to the civil and priestly aristocracy alone.

The fundamental premise on which the code rested was that each of these groups was to be protected by law within its traditional boundaries. And while it stressed the need for the military houses to protect the interests of the non-military elite, it recognized the existence of the military estate as a legitimate bearer of political authority. This conception of a polity based on a balance of authority between civil and military interests was frequently proclaimed as an ideal for the Japanese people.

This principle was rejected briefly in the 1330s when the emperor Go-Daigo (1288–1339) plotted to destroy the Kamakura shogunate and to bring all functions of government, including the military, under his imperial control. Under this plan, civil nobles would serve as military governors and imperial princes were eligible to become shogun. But the times were against such a scheme. Ashikaga Takauji (1305–58), a powerful military governor who had fought against Kamakura for Go-Daigo, turned against the emperor and established in 1336 a new shogunate, this time in the Muromachi section of Kyoto.

The Muromachi shogunate moved in the opposite direction from Go-Daigo's plan. The shogun remained an appointee of the emperor, and the two aristocracies—samurai and court—continued as independent entities. But now civil posts, such as provincial governorships, were taken over completely by military houses, and the Ashikaga family, in an effort to achieve grander status, raised itself into the highest ranks of the court nobility. The third shogun, Yoshimitsu, before his death in 1408, received honors from the court approaching those given only to retired emperors. He even accepted, over the emperor, the designation "King of Japan" from the Ming emperor. The Muromachi shogunate also attempted to reach a cultural level and aesthetic refinement equivalent to that of the court nobility. The Ashikaga rulers' patronage of the arts, in tea ceremony, Nō theatre, and painting, and of garden design and architecture, in the building of such grand residences as the golden and silver pavilions (Gingaku-ji and Kinkaku-ji) and the Palace of Flowers (Hana-no-gosho), were remarkable accomplishments—monuments to the high culture of the new warrior elite.

The Summer Attack on Osaka Castle, 1615. The most prominent symbol of power for the leading daimyo warlords was the multi-storied castle keep. Hideyoshi's cause was defeated with Tokugawa Ieyasu's attack on the Toyotomi castle. (Detail of six-panel screen painting, 17th century. Osaka Castle. Photo © Sekai Bunka Photo.)

Yet there was no usurpation. The hierarchy of warrior families came to parallel the court nobility, but they remained forever samurai, members of a closed social estate.

This was about as far as warrior government could go and still remain under the residual sovereignty of the emperor. During the early sixteenth century, there began to appear in the provinces a fundamentally different type of military lordship. This in time was to lead to the emergence of the daimyo phenomenon whereby military lords acquired total and uninhibited rights over their domains, becoming in the process what we might call warlords.

Daimyo came into existence in a number of ways. Some of the Muromachi period (1392–1568) military governors managed to hold on to portions of their provincial holdings, using power borrowed from the shogun to reduce other military houses in their domains to a condition of vassalage. Others began as small provincial lords, who through superior military capacity, managed to reduce neighboring lords to vassalage.

But whether domains were put together from the top or the bottom, the product was the same. The Sengoku daimyo, as historians now refer to them, were lords of domains within which all superior rights over land were theirs by fact of conquest. Within the domain the daimyo would hold the greater portion of the land, but the rest was given over as fiefs to his vassals. Local administration within the borders of a daimyo domain would be completely divorced from the traditional imperial system of provincial administration. The warlord daimyo was his own authority, administering his domain through his vassals. They in turn had the responsibility of providing military service and of governing the peasant cultivators organized into villages.

The daimyo domains were the product of intense and prolonged warfare, as local military houses contended for domination over men and lands. As of 1550, not all of Japan was neatly divided into compact military domains. Some portions of the country were still fragmented at the village or district level, as local samu-

The Battle of Nagashino, 1575. In Japan's first use of firearms, Oda Nobunaga massed his gunners behind palisades and successfully mowed down the Takeda mounted spearsmen. (Detail of six-panel screen painting, 17th century. Tokugawa Museum of Art. Photo courtesy of the Bunka-chō.)

rai failed to produce a leader capable of asserting authority over them. Elsewhere, daimyo had managed to carve out territories the size of provinces or even more. It was the daimyo of this size and strength that contended for national hegemony during the second half of the sixteenth century.

The larger of the Sengoku daimyo came as close to being independent rulers as Japan was ever to see. The successful Sengoku daimyo were men of sturdy character. All had spent their entire adult lives in battle, in the recruiting of vassal bands, in organizing their followers for military action, in building up the resources of their domains, and in perfecting the machinery of village administration and tax collection. Jesuit missionaries who visited Japan in these years wrote of daimyo as princes or even kings. And indeed daimyo compiled their own domain laws, and even used their own calendars for dating documents. Each daimyo was by necessity a charismatic leader of men, and below him his vassals of various ranks were required to live up to high standards of military performance. Daimyo had attained the capacity to recruit tens of thousands of samurai retainers and their support troops. When the troops of several daimyo were joined under a single command, the resulting armies were huge. The warfare that attended the drive toward unification was the most demanding in Japan's history.

We need not narrate in detail its history, but suffice it to say that the account is commonly told in terms of the exploits of three men: Oda Nobunaga (1534–82), Toyotomi Hideyoshi (1536–98), and Tokugawa Ieyasu (1542–1616). The major turning points in this drive came in 1568, when Nobunaga occupied the imperial capital of Kyoto; 1590, when Hideyoshi destroyed the castle of Odawara and completed the subjugation of the daimyo; 1600, when Ieyasu won the critical battle of Sekigahara that led to the founding of the Edo shogunate; and 1615, when Ieyasu destroyed Osaka castle and with it the last remnants of the Toyotomi cause.

During these years, Japan underwent a transformation in political structure hastened by revolutionary changes in military technology and the capacity to command. Even before Nobunaga made his move on Kyoto, the daimyo had adopted significant changes in military technology. Earlier battles between samurai forces were fought mainly as individual engagements. In the Gempei War of the late twelfth century, the most common warrior type was the horse-riding samurai protected by heavy body armor and skilled in the use of the bow and the sword. Protagonists, before attacking each other, engaged in the ritual of *nanori*, calling out their formal names and previous exploits. They then drew their swords, closed and fought to the finish. The victor took the head of his opponent as evidence in making his claim for reward after the battle.

By the end of the fifteenth century, this pattern of individual combat was being replaced by the use of larger bodies of foot soldiers whose principal weapon was the long spear or halberd. Mounted samurai also gave up the bow for the spear. Castle construction was modified to counter the new military technology. As long as warfare was local and individual in scope, small hilltop defenses into which the local lord and his housemen could take refuge, if attacked, were sufficient for the time. But as the warlord-type warrior made his appearance, castles of larger scale became necessary. No longer could the castle be for defense alone. Into it the daimyo had to gather his military officers, and also bodies of armed unmounted soldiers. The castle had become the command center, a garrisoned strong point, amplified by groups of service personnel, in effect an embryonic castle town.

All of these trends were accelerated by the introduction of firearms from Europe. Oda Nobunaga was the first warlord to take full advantage of firearms in 1575 in the now famous battle of Nagashino, won by his three thousand musketmen shooting in volleys. He pioneered as well with a new style of residential castle built to withstand musket and cannon. Begun in 1576, Azuchi castle, set on a rocky promontory on the shores of Lake Biwa, just east of Kyoto, was barely finished when Nobunaga was killed and the castle destroyed. But Azuchi lives in historic memory as the grandest manifestation of the warlord spirit during the climactic years of the struggle for unification.

Following Nobunaga's death, Hideyoshi, his chief military strategist and loyal general, succeeded to lead the unification of the country. The magnitude of the struggle is revealed in the size of his armies. His conquest of the daimyo of Kyushu in 1588 required the mobilization of some 280,000 men. His last major engagement, the winning of the eight provinces of the Kantō held by the daimyo of Odawara castle, was achieved in 1590 with a force of 100,000 men after a five-month siege. The Kantō provinces were immediately turned over to Tokugawa

Portrait of Honda Tada-katsu (1548–1610). One of the principal daimyo warlords who fought alongside Tokugawa Ieyasu, Tadakatsu was easily recognized in battle and immortalized in history by his impressive antler helmet. (Detail of hanging scroll painting, 16th century. Okazaki Municipal Museum. Photo courtesy of the Bunka-chō.)

Ieyasu, who had provided the largest contingent of troops for the siege. By this move Hideyoshi unwittingly gave Ieyasu the base from which he was to win the hegemony from Hideyoshi's successor. But from 1590 until his death in 1598, Hideyoshi was all powerful. The daimyo of all Japan were his sworn vassals. He could boast that in all Japanese history, he was the first to command the entire country—he used the term *tenka*, or empire.

But Hideyoshi's boast concealed an insecurity which plagued him throughout his career. Having come from a family of less than samurai status, he was denied automatic political legitimation and social status as he won military victory after victory. And so, as a parvenu warlord, he took every opportunity to enhance his image, seeking high office from the court or gaining popular attention by mounting extravagant displays of wealth and military power. His grand open-invitation ten-day tea ceremony in Kyoto in 1587, his flamboyant use of a portable "golden" tea house, his building of the lavish and immense Fushimi and Osaka castles, typify the policy of ostentation which he cultivated. Such was the conspicuous life-style of the warlord daimyo, of whom Hideyoshi was precariously the leader.

It was during the wars of consolidation that a new style of helmet made its appearance. These were the helmets of individual design now known as *kawari kabuto*. What was the motivation behind this phenomenon, and what does this tell us about the men who wore them? Specialists on the subject of Japanese armor do not have ready answers. Much of the literature on the subject is concerned with the analysis of their manufacture and function. And collectors have not gone far beyond the classification of helmets according to the category of the overall design. We remain ignorant of the intended meaning of these designs or the reason why a warrior might have commissioned them.

Prior to the age of Nobunaga and Hideyoshi, the only frontal decoration that adorned the helmet was the set of metalic horn-like prongs riveted to the front. These were called *kuwagata*, or hoe-shaped, attachments. Indeed in the early helmets, the "horns" did take the shape of the iron shoe that served as the cutting point of the standard agricultural hoe. But what function or meaning the *kuwagata* served is not known today, and specialists can only surmise that they were to lend a sense of manliness to the overall look of the helmet. In time, armorers embellished the *kuwagata* by etching designs onto the prongs or by making them longer or wider. The head of the central rivet was also enlarged and given the shape of an animal head or a religious symbol. As such, it acquired the function of a "front-piece," or *maedate*. But there was not much more that could be done to make a more forceful statement. The new style was obliged to make a clean break with tradition by discarding the *kuwagata* and *maedate* and using the entire helmet bowl as a base on which to attach constructions of almost unlimited variety.

It was on the battlefield, of course, that the spirit of the age of military consolidation was most explicitly displayed. Near-contemporary paintings of battle scenes show vividly the new patterns of command and the new strategies for the placement of fighting units. Screen paintings of climactic battles like Nagashino (1575), Nagakute (1584), Sekigahara (1600), and Osaka (1614–15) are especially revealing. In the battles in the open countryside, daimyo and their field commanders are generally shown occupying high ground on horseback and wearing highly-colorful armor, topped with helmets of distinctive shape. Far from trying to keep out of sight or in a protected location, they appeared to be seeking maximum visibility. Surrounded by mounted officers, each in his own conspicuous armor and helmet and displaying banners and other identifying insignias, the command post seems to be in active touch with units of unmounted soldiers dressed in uniform livery.

The battle strategy was clearly based on the movement of armed units. The daimyo gesturing with battle-fan or baton was the strategist, and the power that emanated from his helmet filled the space between he and his men. Although his location made him a prime target for the sniper's bullet, the range and accuracy of the musket were still not that much to be feared. By contrast, the siege of a castle, as seen in screen paintings of the battle for Osaka castle, gave rise to a more crowded and confused environment. In such a situation, the helmet served to establish immediate recognition for the wearer.

Characteristic of these fanciful helmets was that all were designed independently of the body armor. Furthermore, the attached forms were not meant to enhance the protective capacity of the helmet, though of course the protective functions were not neglected. Beneath the sculptural decoration, constructed of *harikake* (laminated paper or leather), the iron helmet bowl at the base continued to improve. Emphasis was placed on iconography alone. And for the warrior on the battlefield, the capacity to exert a personal image of power with which to meet the enemy or raise the spirits of his men was all important.

T he helmets selected for this exhibition are representative of the variety of helmets in existence today. Most of them date from the early Edo period. Each presumably makes a statement on behalf of the original wearer, though the symbolism is not always clear. Some were simply graphic displays of the warrior patron's family crest. Others had religious meaning and expressed some aspect of the wearer's belief, or invited some hoped-for talismanic power. And still others, it would seem, simply displayed an aura of ferocity or even whimsy.

As active warlords, men like Hideyoshi or Ieyasu appear to have worn many different helmets. They also gave *kabuto* as tokens of favor. Other daimyo have gone down in history identified by a single distinctive helmet design. Katō Kiyomasa (1562–1611), one of Hideyoshi's lead generals in the Korean invasion,

*Part of a daimyo travel procession en route to Edo for alternative attendance duty (*sankin kōtai*). High officials rode horseback; those of the lower rank were on foot. Note the somber faces of the daimyo's attendants. Each samurai was distinguished by his family crest, visible on the back and sleeves of his outer garment. (Detail of handscroll painting, 17th century. Tokugawa Museum of Art. Photo © Sekai Bunka Photo.)*

is usually depicted in a helmet that simulated a tall court hat on which was painted a red rising sun. Honda Tadakatsu (1548–1610) is famous for his helmet displaying large deer antlers. Kuroda Nagamasa (1568–1623) is identified with a helmet showing large stylized water buffalo horns protruding from either side. Yet another daimyo, Date Masamune (1567–1636) of Sendai, became identified with a helmet capped by a large tilted crescent moon, while the Hosokawa house of Kumamoto adorned its helmets with long pheasant tail feathers.

The making of suits of armor in the traditional style and with them the designing of special helmets continued into the late Edo period. As can be seen in the collection before us, most of these are for parade use only. With the achievement of peace under the Tokugawa house, the emphasis was placed on restraint and conformity. The Edo shogunate made every effort to prevent the outbreak of warfare within the country. The hierarchy of rank among daimyo and lesser samurai was carefully defined and constantly reinforced through public display. Rank determined the size of residences, the width of residential entrances, the number of retainers or of men at arms, the style of clothing and even the varieties of food.

For the samurai estate, one-of the most influential practices that forced conformity to sumptuary regulations was the practice of alternate attendance at the shogun's court at Edo. Daimyo were obliged to travel between their own castle headquarters and Edo so as to be available to the shogun every other year or half-year. They were expected to travel in a style appropriate to their rank, so that the travel procession was regulated down to the smallest detail. The trained eye could immediately tell the identity of the daimyo on the road simply by observing the number and style of ceremonial emblems carried at the head of the procession, the style of the daimyo's palanquin, the number of his road attendants, and the like. Pertinent information about the daimyo was conveniently available in the *bukan*, or daimyo directories, of the time. The Sengoku daimyo had vied with each other in their extravagant displays, dressing their retainers in colorful liveries, and in the number of troops they added to their entourage. The daimyo of the Edo period had to live within the shogunate's restrictive sumptuary regulations.

The Edo period travel procession, like the battle array of the Sengoku samurai, was deeply symbolic. Display of family crests, of prudently uniformed attendants, and the proper form of emblems, reinforced the contours of a rigidly defined status system, a monument to the status quo. Esoterically designed helmets may have been worn but only on ceremonial occasions and then only in an effort to recapture the spirit of the past. For the Edo-period samurai, advancement through performance on the battlefield was no longer possible. As with the firearms that had won the peace, the spirit of adventure and conquest had to be put aside. The new motto set before the samurai, "letters and military arts," was appropriate for a class of urban bureaucrats, and that is what the samurai were fast becoming. For them, innovation was found in the designing of new administrative techniques and in the reconstruction of the past—as in the discovery of a warrior ethic in the idealized form of *bushidō* and in the revival of scholarship on military history, as with the publication of the first history of arms and armor, the *Honchō Gunkikō*. The warlord world of the sixteenth century could speak to Japan at the start of its modern era only in a disembodied form as a philosophy of military preparedness or a regimen of individual self-discipline. The contemporary search for historic roots has directed attention to the *kawari kabuto* as a rich source of insight into the thought-world of Japan's pre-modern military elite.

KAWARI KABUTO:
JAPAN'S EXTRAORDINARY HELMETS

Yoshihiko Sasama, Iwao Fujimoto, and Yūichi Hiroi
Translated by Richard Gage

The earliest surviving examples of armor in Japan are those artifacts excavated from the great tumuli of the fifth century. Remarkably complete armor and richly adorned arms together with clay tomb figurines, called *haniwa*, that depict fully-equipped warriors, provide a rather clear image of the armor in the "Age of Gods." These prove that the people of Japan manufactured armor from metal. But the production of armor in general—notably helmets and other protective coverings of hides and woven vines—no doubt predates that age. It is impossible to know, however, how this ancient armor made of perishable organic materials actually looked.

Armor dating from the fifth century is generally classified into two types. The first, called *keikō*, is made of small iron plates bound together with tanned leather thongs or cords, and is in the tradition of armor worn by mounted warriors of the Asian continent. Like other elements of continental culture which reached Japan, this kind of armor was altered and adapted by the Japanese to suit their own needs and tastes. The second type, called *tankō*, was a breast plate similar to those of ancient Greek and Roman armor, but once again adjusted to Japanese needs and preferences.

With frequent alterations and improvements, these two types of armor continued to be used until the tenth century. By the eighth century or so, however, the iron-plate *keikō* ceased to be produced for battle and was relegated instead to ceremonial use by the imperial court. Highly intricate, fragile and rather heavy, *keikō*—made up of eight hundred or so small iron plates—was replaced during this time by another lighter version better suited for battle.

In about the tenth century, two new styles or armor emerged that replaced earlier *keikō* and *tankō* modes. *Yoroi* was designed in response to the needs of the mounted warrior who battled with bow and arrow; the lighter *dōmaru*, so-called because it enclosed the trunk of the body (*dō*) in a round (*maru*) form, was used by warriors requiring greater freedom of movement on the ground. (In older sources, the *dōmaru* is referred to as a *haramaki*, a term in use today that means "belly wrapping.")

Two helmets dating from the sixth century excavated from burial mounds in Kumamoto Prefecture. These helmets, composed of several iron plates riveted together to form a hemisphere, are among the earliest examples of Japanese armor. (Bunka-chō, Tokyo. Photo courtesy of the Collection.)

Through the battles of the twelfth through fourteenth century, the manufacture of *yoroi* and *dōmaru* were gradually improved and refined. Eventually, however, the heavier *yoroi* was replaced by a combination of *dōmaru* and helmet. By the fifteenth and sixteenth century, only high-ranking warriors with a proclivity for majestic display actually wore *yoroi*; the rest of the soldiery preferred the lighter style.

The development of the Japanese helmet (*kabuto*) parallels the evolution of the traditional lamellar cuirass. The earliest helmets are of Mongolian shape; they are rounded and conical in form and built of vertical plates surmounted by an inverted semi-spherical cup. Helmets of the tenth and eleventh century consisted of a simple low bowl with a hole at the tip for the warrior's queue to pass through. The bowl, lined with leather and lacquered, was made up of single plates of iron with applied ridges, or built up of eight to twelve plates. It was adorned with large conical rivet heads arranged in rows up the sides of the helmet bowl. A neck-guard (*shikoro*) and lateral backturned flaps (*fukigaeshi*) were attached. A ring in the rear was for small flags to identify the warrior, and a heavy silk cord was used to tie the helmet under the chin. The front bore an ornament, usually an insignia or auspicious motif of some kind (*maedate*). Generals, however, decorated the front of their helmets with hoe-shaped, horn-like attachments called *kuwagata*. Though their meaning is not clear, the *kuwagata* lent majesty and distinction to the *kabuto*.

Anew kind of armor and helmet appeared in the sixteenth century, largely inspired by European styles that were introduced by way of Portuguese, Spanish, and Dutch traders, and devised as well in response to the new class of military leaders. During a century of civil war, known as the Sengoku era, rapid improvements in the cuirass and helmet were demanded for greater ease of mobility, and for the enhancement of a leader's image on the battlefield. The new armor was called *tōsei-gusoku*.

The most outstanding change in the armor of the sixteenth century, however, was the emergence of the *kawari kabuto*, literally "extraordinary helmets." These unique designs were the expression of the new class of warriors, performing battle in large groups on open fields. In this often confused fighting situation, the warriors needed to distinguish their identity—from ally and enemy—in some conspicuous fashion. If victorious, the self-made leaders flaunted their power by asserting an image of splendor, might, and bold individuality. Striking pieces of ornament thus began to appear on the armor parts, specifically, on the helmet. With the simplification and rationalization of the protective helmet-bowl, it became increasingly fashionable to decorate the helmet in a majestic, even menacing, way. The most startling examples of such extraordinary helmets are presented in this exhibition.

Essentially designed for the traditional function of protecting one's head, *kawari kabuto* nonetheless seem to emphasize art and craftsmanship at the expense of bodily defense. At times, these helmets exhibit forms that seem to run counter to the very nature of a helmet, and appear as if they were created for some very different, "unhelmetlike" purpose. In fact, *kawari kabuto* were made with the idea of calling attention to the existence of one person: the wearer.

While the standard Japanese helmet had traditionally been hemisperical, made by riveting together numerous slender iron plates, the helmets in this exhibition, while basically the same structure, have superficial ornamental accretions that

Takeda Shingen moon-viewing at Suruga Bay. Shingen (1521–1573) was a powerful daimyo of the Sengoku era with a wide sphere of influence in central Japan. In 1571, he joined a conspiracy to destroy the growing power of Oda Nobunaga and his allies. Shingen marched against and defeated young Tokugawa Ieyasu at Mikata-ga-hara, Ieyasu's only major defeat in his long career. This print depicts Shingen seated on a camp stool in full armor enjoying the magnificent Suruga Bay, long noted for its view of Mt. Fuji. Shingen is wearing the famous helmet of the Takeda clan which features a horned demon with a lion's mane. (Woodblock print by Yoshitoshi, 19th century. R.B. Caldwell Collection. Photo courtesy of the American Foundation of Far Eastern Art.)

make them entirely different from their predecessors. This is the source of the name that later scholars and fanciers—not of course the sixteenth-century people who made and wore them—have given these helmets: *kawari kabuto* from *kawari* to change or be different, and *kabuto* or helmet.

In the sixteenth century, when these extraordinary helmets first began appearing, Japan was undergoing social upheaval. Actual power was all that mattered in an age when an old establishment of social classes was crumbling and a new culture was being built. The entire nation was forced to endure a period of bloody struggle that was finally calmed by the power of two great military leaders and political unifiers, Oda Nobunaga (1534–82) and Toyotomi Hideyoshi (1536–98). The new culture that came into being after the new order was established is called Momoyama, after a castle Hideyoshi built for himself on Peach Hill (Momoyama), south of modern Kyoto. It was a splendid, colorful culture incorporating exotic elements of European civilization, but it was nonetheless regulated by a newly formed system of social classes—at whose pinnacle was the samurai. In art, architecture, fashion, and thought, originality was prized. The new military aristocracy set extraordinary examples for a wholly-different and modern culture. In this climate, inspired by such license, the *kawari kabuto* were born.

The essential force behind the emergence of Japan's so-called extraordinary helmets, however, lies in the very simple desire cultivated by the new class of warriors—to be conspicuous. Just as the avant-garde of many post-war societies have adopted eccentric dress and hair styles as a means of revolution and creative expression, so the samurai of the sixteenth century, not wishing to be swallowed up in a mob of uniformly attired soldiers wore flamboyant helmets designed and produced according to individual specification. However the motive of the avant-garde youth and that of the Japanese warrior are different. The avant-garde youth employs extravagance as a symbol of rejection of social responsibility. In contrast, the Japanese warrior of the past donned such gear as flamboyant helmets because he wanted to expose himself to the general eye. This habit served to check any violations he might feel inclined to commit against the established moral code of responsibilities and honor which had evolved over the many years during which the warrior class had held a position of importance in society. By being conspicuous, he was above scorn and contempt.

No two of these helmets are alike, and the variety of their thematic images is immense. Among the most favored motifs, however, are those connected with religion and specifically with Shinto gods and various members of the Buddhist pantheon. On the field of battle, the warrior came face to face with death. Under these circumstances, it is understandable that he should wish to express faith in supernatural beings in the hope of obtaining their protection. In simpler form, such expressions were no more than inscribing the name of a god or Buddha on the helmet (see cat. no. 44), or inserting an amulet into the headgear. More in the spirit of *kawari kabuto*, however, were those whose entire shape was devoted to the protrayal of a religious image. (See cat. no. 24) Reasons for wishing to adorn the helmet with religious figures reveal the samurai's attitude toward battle and death. First, the warrior no doubt wanted to be transformed into the divinity gracing his helmet and thus obtain supernatural powers to defeat his enemy. Second, the god or Buddha on the helmet symbolized an offering made in the name of the men the warrior wearing it might kill. In addition, the god was something to which the warrior could cling in the event that he himself was struck down. Designs of this kind were a kind of repentance for the sin inherent in killing. The most outstanding reasons, as with the crosses born high by the Crusaders, were justification of his own acts through faith and the menacing of the enemy through the borrowed form of a divine being.

Symbolic representation of natural phenomena, such as mountains, waves, and whirlpools was another motif the military elite fancied for the adornment of the *kawari kabuto*. (See cat. nos.11, 53, 69, and 70.) The great powers of nature inspired the samurai to achieve equal majesty and force, and the drama of their forms were impressive totems.

Choices of other thematic motifs were determined by a less power-oriented philosophy. A good many *kawari-kabuto* were fashioned in the image of elegant hats and crowns of the distant past. *Eboshi*, the lacquered headgear traditionally worn by courtiers and high-ranking samurai, inspired such helmets (see cat. nos. 3, 12, and 30). Others were inspired by classical Chinese hats worn by court-officials (see cat. no. 4), while still others copied the various felt hats that were introduced by the Europeans in the sixteenth century (see cat. nos. 43 and 76). Hoods were another type of headgear transformed for the helmet. Called *zukin*, they were adopted in various styles for the helmet (see cat. nos. 7, 12, 50, and 51). Some simulate hair styles (see cat. no. 66), while others replicate *tenugui* and other kinds of head wrappings (see cat. nos. 6, 13, and 71).

Animal and sea creatures were other subjects for the new helmet. Often auspicious animals such as the hare, tortoise, or mythical lion were incorporated (see cat. nos. 13, 15, 57); frequently, animals that symbolized strength and ferocity were fantasized, such as the bear (see cat. no. 32) or the bull (see cat. no. 17). Shellfish, such as the lobster, crab, and various types of mollusks, were favored by the samurai because the shells symbolized their own armor. The helmets were depicted at times with great realism, and at other times were totally abstracted.

Plants and vegetables also topped the helmet forms. Some, like leaves of the holly tree or *kashiwa* oak, were chosen for their auspicious meanings (see cat. no. 29 and 41). Others, like the pumpkin, were chosen simply because they were exotic looking (see cat. no. 52). Still others, like the eggplant, were chosen for no special reason at all (see cat. no. 60).

Everyday objects and ordinary articles were occasionally the subject for a sculpture to cap the warrior's head. In the spirit of the *kabuki no jidai*, an epoch which celebrated the bizarre, odd, and the funny, in good taste, the military elite put the least expected and most conspicuous things on their heads. Whatever the form, and whatever the inspiration, the important thing was to have a helmet unlike all others.

F or a better appreciation of the fine work of the *kawari kabuto*, it is necessary to understand the materials and structures of their composition. The helmet-bowl, the base for the decorative form and the protective headgear, is made of thin strips of iron hammered into curves and riveted together to form a hemispherical or conical shape. This construction is no different than the simple headgear of pre-sixteenth century Japan. The decorative formations are then attached or built upon this base.

The sculptural shapes which surmount the *kabuto* are made in one or a combination of four ways: hammered iron, carved wood, bamboo, or lacquered *harikake* made of paper or leather.

Portrait of Kuroda Naga-masa (1568–1623). Mounted in full armor, Nagamasa is shown wearing a helmet in the shape of Ichi-no-tani Canyon, a favorite style among warriors of the sixteenth century. Nagamasa was one of the great warriors of the Momoyama and early Edo periods. He fought in over thirty battles, and was not defeated once. (Detail of hanging scroll painting, 17th century. Fukuoka City Museum. Photo courtesy of the Bunka-chō).

Hammered thin and formed, iron is used for the smaller decorations which cap certain helmets. Because of its heaviness, it could not be used for the larger, more elaborate forms. (See cat. nos. 25, 46, 58, and 65.)

Wood is used to portray the masks of Shinto and Buddhist dieties, and for the fine carving of such forms as antlers and horns. The wood is often lacquered, and sometimes finished in gold or silver leaf. (See cat. nos. 24 and 57). Other ornaments are made of finely split, woven bamboo finished in lacquer.

The majority of the *kawari kabuto* are constructed of *harikake*, a material composed of laminated paper or leather. It is so-called because the paper or leather is first pasted (*haru*) over wooden forms (*kakeru* means to "put over" or "cover"), then dried, and removed in a method similar to the one by which papier maché objects are produced.

The paper used for *harikake* is made of fibers from the bark of the paper mulberry (*kōzo*). This tough paper is then pasted in many layers, as many as ten or more, on a wooden matrix that is applied with a linen cloth so as to prevent deformation. The layers of paper on linen are allowed to dry, and then removed from the wooden form. Its shape is then that which will surmount the helmet.

To protect the paper from damp and rot, to refine the form, and to enhance the beauty of the surface, the *harikake* form is then lacquered. Numerous base coats of lacquer mixed with powdered, fired earth are first applied, followed by coats of top-grade lacquer. Final coats might involve decorative techniques such as *maki-e* or *gindami*, whereby metallic dust and pigments are sprinkled in a design on the damp lacquer.

Harikake is also made with tanned leather. The leather is first softened by soaking in water, and then it is pressed and hammered against wooden molds. Complicated forms are divided into sections that are later joined and sewn together. When dried, the leather is removed from the form and coated first with a mixture of powdered, fired earth and lacquer, and finally with high-quality lacquer. The Japanese term for works made of lacquered leather is *shippi*.

A number of helmets are designed in iron, or with attachments of some kind of metal or other. As lacquer does not adhere readily to metals, a coat is applied to the metal object which is then heated to about thirty degrees centigrade. This forms a bond between the two. Further coats of lacquer may then be applied to the original one. This process is complicated, however, because lacquer will not dry at temperatures above eighty degrees centigrade.

The natural colors of lacquer range from golden to reddish browns. Traditionally, it is made black with additions of soot produced by burning pine or oil. In the fifteenth century, however, it became customary to use iron powder or powdered ferric hydroxide for this purpose. Cinnabar, or mercuric sulfide (the red powder left when mercury is evaporated), is used to produce vermilion. Various other pigments are employed to tint lacquer other hues.

Not all soldiers in Japan wore such extravagant headgear. The rank and file were outfitted in more or less uniform armor and carried uniform banners and emblems to make it possible to identify friend from foe. Leaders, however, especially those who prided themselves on their valor, sported *kawari-kabuto*, which were a kind of privilege of status. Although it may be difficult to prove the provenance of the helmets displayed in this exhibition, it is certain that all of them belonged to warriors of the first rank. They represent a high level of art, design, and craftsmanship, and express—in unique form—the spirit of the age.

CATALOGUE

1. Armor with helmet in shape of auspicious motif

Edo period, 18th century
Kinkarakawa leather, lacquer on iron, silk cords (armor);
iron, black lacquer and gold and silver *maki-e* on *harikake* (helmet)
Height of helmet: 26.3 cm.
Takatsu Kobunka Kaikan, Kyoto

The construction of this helmet is typical of *kawari kabuto*. Its bowl, made of iron, serves as protective armor for the head and as a base for the sculptural design which rises from it, made of *harikake* and finished in black lacquer. Ornamented with designs and characters of good fortune in gold and silver *maki-e*, a decorative technique whereby sprinkled gold and silver powder is applied to lacquered designs while still damp, the magnificent form which tops the helmet is an abstract representation of *noshi*, the long strips of dried abalone traditionally served with *sake* on ceremonial occasions. Because their length and toughness suggest longevity, abalone strips came to be used as decoration in the presentation of gifts. The face guard is of hammered and tempered iron finished in vermilion lacquer.

An inscription on the inner surface of the cuirass relates that this set of armor was commissioned by Iwai Yoshichika lord of Echigo (modern Niigata Prefecture) and a member of the illustrious Matsudaira family, relatives of the ruling Tokugawa shoguns. Decorative and highly-refined armor of this kind was possible in the Edo period, when a generally prevailing peace rendered more functional armor unnecessary and affluence and prosperity among the upper classes inspired lavish patronage of the costly metal, lacquer, and textile arts. Such armor and helmets were typically commissioned by high-ranking lords of the day for display in festival processions, parades of state, ceremonies, and other occasions of rank and pomp. Its fine craftsmanship and bold design express the very best work in this art of the period.

2. Helmet in the form of a roll of silk

Momoyama period, late 16th century
Iron, black lacquer on *harikake*
Height: 35.7 cm.
Takatsu Kobunka Kaikan, Kyoto

This helmet is a remarkable example of the sculptural and theatrical forms fancied by the leading warriors of the Momoyama period, a time when individualism blazed. The crown of the helmet is embossed with expressive lines that depict the wrinkles of a mighty forehead. The wide form rising above the crown, suggesting a full-blown sail, represents a roll of silk.

Everyday utensils and common objects with no specific auspicious meaning were often incorporated as motifs for helmet designs during this age. Outstanding examples are the use of a straw grain-bag (see cat. no. 61) and a rice or soup bowl (see cat. no. 42); parts of a kettle, a kettle's tripod, a funnel, and a spindle were also used.

3. Filigree helmet in the form of a "windblown" courtier's hat
Late Muromachi period, 16th century
Gold leaf on leather
Height: 18.9 cm.
Uesugi Shrine, Yamagata Prefecture

This helmet, said to have been worn by Uesugi Kenshin (1530-78), lord of Echigo (modern Niigata Prefecture), is made in the form of a *kazaori eboshi,* the "windblown" type of the traditional headgear worn by courtiers and high-ranking samurai. Designed as the ceremonial headdress for court nobles of the Heian period (794-1185), these lacquered hats were later adopted by samurai who wore them over their hair, which was pulled back and tied in a top knot with a cord, with the helmet then surmounting the entire headgear. With changes in hair fashion and the manufacture of helmets after the thirteenth century, the samurai abandoned this use of *eboshi.* In time, the hats came to symbolize the image of the classical warrior of such epic battles as the Gosannen (1083-87) and Gempei (1183-85) wars.

Designed in the shape of an *eboshi* turned down from the crown into a three-cornered form (thus "windblown"), this headpiece was probably worn as an ornament over a protective helmet. It is leather filigreed in the *karakusa* pattern, a scrolling vine motif (not unlike the Western arabesque) of Chinese origin that was popular in the Japanese textile and decorative arts. It is covered in gold leaf and inscribed in the center with the character *mu,* a Zen Buddhist philosophical term. It is the concept a Zen-affiliated warrior would meditate upon in facing death; that it appears on Uesugi Kenshin's helmet suggests his own identification—which was indeed devout—with Zen.

4. Helmet in the shape of Chinese-style headgear
Momoyama period, late 16th century
Iron, black lacquer on *harikake*
Height: 28.6 cm.
Collection of Tadao Nishiyama, Saitama Prefecture

In the late sixteenth century, helmets patterned after the ceremonial lacquer hats called *tōkanmuri*, traditionally worn by high-ranking Chinese officials, were fashionable among the new warrior elite. Exotic and stately, such helmets were coveted by the samurai.

The helmet-bowl consists of five iron plates, and additional iron has been used to create the rising section in the back. Black-lacquered *harikake* is attached to this base, and embossed on the helmet's front are two stylized eyebrows. The neck guard (*shikoro*), which can contract and expand, is constructed of five ranks of thin iron plates laced together with white leather thongs. Although simple, the form of this helmet is a skillful composition of curving lines and volumes.

5. Helmet with decorations in the shape of the water plantain
Momoyama period, late 16th century
Iron, black lacquer on *harikake*
Height: 20.1 cm.
Collection of Fusao Tomoda, Kyoto

Among the forms after which many *kawari kabuto* of the sixteenth century were patterned, various kinds of flowers, trees, fruits, and vegetables were favored. This design of two water plantain leaves illustrates how such plant forms were typically abstracted to adorn the warrior's helmet. The water plantain, called *omodaka*, was introduced to Japan from China and became a popular motif in Japanese art. The elegance of its long tapered leaves inspired numerous patterns especially in lacquer, metal, and textile arts, and was used as well for some insignia and crests.

The helmet bowl is of the *hōdan* or bullet-shape type, so-called for its elongated form. The bowl is constructed of twelve iron plates and is surmounted by the form which is made of *harikake*. The sheen of the black lacquer accentuates the outlines to enhance the beauty of the three-dimensional forms.

6. Helmet in form of folded *tenugui* cloth
Momoyama period, late 16th century
Iron
Height: 16.3 cm.
Collection of Hajime Fujita, Okayama Prefecture

It has long been a custom in Japan to use the *tenugui,* an oblong cloth having the standard lengths of some fourteen inches long and some twelve inches wide, for all kinds of utilitarian purposes from washcloth to head-band. This untraditional helmet represents a *tenugui* folded and placed on top of the head, in a style that is typically worn in Japan.

The construction of this helmet represents a departure in the manufacture and technology of late sixteenth-century iron-work with the use of rivets to piece together the five iron plates. Helmets made in this way and patterned after the *tenugui* were produced by armorers from Saika in the province of Kii (modern Wakayama Prefecture). This one is signed by Saika Yoshihisa.

7. Helmet in the shape of a four-cornered hood
Momoyama period, late 16th century
Iron, black lacquer on *harikake*, gilt metal
Height: 27.2 cm.
Collection of Tadao Yoshii, Osaka

The use of hats, hoods, and other everyday headgear for helmet motifs was popular among fashionable warriors of the Sengoku era, the period when central administrative powers of the shogunal court collapsed and provincial warlords battled each other for local advantage and ultimate supremacy. Warriors vying for leadership took to wearing the most conspicuous and unusual helmets to attract attention to themselves and to exert a charismatic presence. This towering helmet represents a *sumi-zukin*, a hood shaped like a four-cornered bag, tied in front of the brow. Though without any specific meaning, this helmet is impressive by its very size and shape.

8. Helmet shaped as the elongated head of the God of Longevity
Momoyama period, late 16th century
Gindami on iron
Height: 34.0 cm.
Collection of Tadamasa Mitsuhashi, Tokyo

The God of Longevity, know as Jurōjin in Japanese, is one of the Seven Gods of Good Fortune introduced from China and popular in Japan. He is traditionally depicted as a tall old man in the dress of a scholar, with an elongated head. This helmet, made of several iron plates, is designed after the god's most salient attribute.

The surface is produced by a decorative lacquer technique, called *gindami*. Damp lacquer is sprinkled with silver dust, allowed to dry, and coated with lacquer again. When the surface is polished, it takes on a silvery sheen. This imposing helmet must have been visible across the battlefield when the sun struck the silver dust and gleamed bright.

9. Helmet in the shape of Ichi-no-tani Canyon
Momoyama period, late 16th century
Iron, black lacquer on *harikake*
Height: 28.7 cm.
Collection of Fusao Tomoda, Kyoto

Ichi-no-tani is a rocky valley in the
Tekkai mountains to the west of Kobe
in Hyogo Prefecture. It is famed as the
site where, in 1184, the celebrated warrior
Minamoto Yoshitsune galloped down the
valley walls to defeat the Taira clan and so
win one of the greatest military victories
in Japanese history. Helmets fashioned
after the precipitous walls of Ichi-no-tani
were popular among the sixteenth-century
warlords, who sought a glory equal to
Yoshitsune's. (See cat. nos. 26 and 36.) The
concise abstraction of this landscape form
is an outstanding work on the part of the
armorer for its large frontal area would
be menacing to friend and foe alike.

10. Helmet ornamented with the Buddhist wish-granting jewel
Momoyama period, late 16th century
Iron, gilt copper
Height: 26.0 cm.
Collection of Saburō Makita, Tokyo

Buddhist and Shinto emblems were often incorporated into the designs of *kawari kabuto*. Like the Christian cross born by the Crusaders, the warriors of Japan used religious symbols to justify through faith their acts on the battlefield and to overwhelm the enemy through the borrowed power of a divine being. This helmet, an outstanding example of its kind, features a gilt-copper flaming cintāmani jewel, which in Buddhist tradition is thought to have the mystical power of granting all wishes.

The production of this complicated helmet demanded the greatest level of technical skill. Composed of sixty-two iron plates arranged in a conical form, the numerous rivets holding the plates in place are thought to resemble sleet. The iron has not been lacquered in order to reveal the excellence of the metal work. This type of exposed iron surface is called *kanasabi-ji*.

11. Helmet with double-whirlpool designs
Early Edo period, 17th century
Iron, black, lacquer on *harikake*, and hair
Height: 23.5 cm.
Collection of Tatsuo Nakamura, Kyoto

This helmet, with two whirlpools that look like giant dragonfly eyes, is said to have been part of a suit of armor worn by Katō Akitomo (d. 1683), daimyo of Minaguchi (modern Shiga Prefecture) during the early decades of Tokugawa rule. Resting on top of a domed helmet-bowl made up of five iron plates, the *harikake* composition with its curving and geometric forms gives an impression of great freshness and fluidity.

Natural phenomena were favorite motifs for helmet designs. The power of great mountains such as Fuji—or of ocean waves, fire, turbulent clouds—were often incorporated into fantastic shapes to surmount the warrior's head. The whirlpool, a dangerous zone against whose force one is powerless, is abstracted here in bold, even modernist design and demonstrates a high level of craftsmanship.

12. Helmet in the form of a Zen priest's hood

Early Edo period, early 17th century
Iron, black and red lacquer on *harikake*
Height: 23.4 cm.
Fukuoka City Museum, Fukuoka Prefecture

Said to have been worn by the Kyushu daimyo Kuroda Nagamasa (1568–1623), this helmet is shaped like the heavy cloth hood worn by Zen priests, called a *mōsu*. Executed in *harikake*, it rests on top of a domed helmet-bowl. The treatment is very realistic and depicts the hood as it would appear swept back in the wind. This form gives the impression of motion and charge. The brow, depicted in vermilion lacquer, is embossed with expressive eyebrows.

Kuroda Nagamasa was one of the principal daimyo of the Momoyama period. He played a major role in the military campaigns which lead to the unification of Japan after a century of civil wars and to the victorious supremacy of the Tokugawa shogunate, in 1615. Lord of the vast Chikuzen province (modern Fukuoka Prefecture) in Kyushu, Nagamasa served the all-powerful Toyotomi Hideyoshi in the 1587 campaign to subjugate rival daimyo clans in Kyushu and in the 1592 invasion of Korea. He later sided with Tokugawa Ieyasu, challenger to Hideyoshi's lineage, and fought in the critical Sekigahara (1600) and Osaka castle (1615) battles. He represents the kind of daimyo for whom the spectacular *kawari kabuto* were invented.

13. Helmet with a rabbit
Early Edo period, early 17th century
Iron, leather, gold leaf and black lacquer on *harikake*, red lacquer on wood
Height: 30.1 cm.
Collection of Tadao Nishiyama, Saitama Prefecture

The hare (*usagi*) is one of the familiar animals of Japanese forklore. One of the hare's most popular mythical associations is longevity. The Japanese traditionally see in the moon an image of the animal pounding the elixir of life. Emblems of longevity, such as the God of Longevity (see cat. nos. 8 and 27) and abalone strips (see cat. no. 1), were favored auspicious motifs the warrior incorporated into his crown of defense when entering battle and facing possible death.

The domed helmet-bowl is made of iron plates on top of which is a leather version of the *mattō*, a kind of head-wrapping. The surface of this wrapped form is covered in gold leaf, and the knotted cord in front is finished in black lacquer. The hare, with exaggerated ears, is carved of wood and lacquered red.

14. Helmet in the form of an open clam shell
Early Edo period, early 17th century
Iron, black lacquer on leather
Height: 40.4 cm.
Collection of Tadao Nishiyama, Saitama Prefecture

The stylized form of clam shells attached to this iron-plated, domed helmet-bowl are big enough to resemble elephant ears. The upward, extending curves of the black-lacquered shells seem to alter with shifts in angle and light, lending the impression of motion.

Shellfish were among the motifs warlords fancied for their *kawari kabuto*, for such creatures wore, like the warrior, a "suit of armor." Beyond any such symbolism, however, helmets such as this one were more likely created for the desire to exert—through the most unexpected and conspicuous attire—a distinct image of power.

15. Helmet ornamented with deer antlers and mythical lion
Early Edo period, early 17th century
Red lacquer on iron, gold leaf on wood, glass
Height: 21.3 cm.
Suntory Museum of Art, Tokyo

This helmet is said to be part of a suit of armor worn by Toyotomi Hidetsugu (1568–95), nephew and adopted son of Toyotomi Hideyoshi, the military ruler who played a vitally important role in the unification of Japan in the late sixteenth century. At the height of Hideyoshi's power, just when he had successfully subjugated all daimyo in Japan to his vassalage, he adopted Hidetsugu as heir and named him regent. But shortly thereafter, Hidetsugu fell into a state of dissipation and lost Hideyoshi's favor. When Hideyoshi heard that his heir was plotting the capture of Osaka castle, he banished Hidetsugu and in 1595 ordered him to commit suicide. Hidetsugu's children and more than thirty women in his service were subsequently executed.

The main body of this helmet, composed of six iron plates and coated in red lacquer, might be fashioned after an *eboshi*, the ceremonial headgear worn by court nobles and high-ranking samurai, or it might be a so-called bullet-shaped helmet, the kind inspired by European prototypes. Antlers of the deer, which is sacred in Shinto and an emblem of longevity in Japan, have been carved in wood and covered in gold leaf. The horned head of a Japanese mythical lion crowns the helmet, as if guarding its wearer by terrifying any advancers. The head is carved in wood, gold-leafed, and inset with glass eyes.

16. Helmet in the form of a straw hood adorned with ferns
Early Edo period, early 17th century
Chestnut-colored lacquer on iron, gold leaf on wire and leather
Height: 26.5 cm.
Ueda Municipal Museum, Nagano Prefecture

This helmet is part of a suit of armor said to have been worn by the opulent daimyo Sengoku Hidehisa (1551–1614), lord of Mino (modern Gifu Prefecture) and a loyal warlord in Toyotomi Hideyoshi's service. Iron is hammered and finely embossed to form a replica of the *wara-zukin*, a hood woven from dried rice or wheat straw. The embossing of the metal required mature technical skill. The flanking ornaments, which recall the *kuwagata* horn-like attachments on early Japanese helmets, represent the kind of fern (*shida*) used for decorations on auspicious occasions. They are made of leather and wire, and covered in gold leaf.

65

17. Helmet in the shape of a cow's head
Early Edo period, early 17th century
Iron, lacquer on *harikake*, silver leaf on wood
Height: 40.3 cm.
Collection of Hajime Fujita, Okayama Prefecture

Cattle horns were a favorite form with which warriors of sixteenth and seventeenth century Japan adorned their helmets. Menacing and majestic, the protruding horns could not but lend an image of strength.

This bold and fantastic piece is somewhat different from most others made in Japan during this period in that *harikake* has been used to replicate the bone structure of a cow's head, from which the horns project to the right and left. The head is finished in light-brown lacquer, which is textured with fine lines produced by having been tapped all over while wet with a cloth-wrapped ball of cotton. The roughly-carved wooden horns are black-lacquered and finished in silver leaf.

18. Helmet shaped as rabbit ears
Early Edo period, early 17th century
Iron, black lacquer on leather
Height: 41.8 cm.
Collection of Fusao Tomoda, Kyoto

This helmet was worn by the daimyo Tōdō Takatora (1556–1630), lord of Iyo (modern Ehime Prefecture). Takatora served the ruling warlords, Oda Nobunaga and his successor Toyotomi Hideyoshi, during the crucial years of military campaigns toward national unification. Takatora commanded fleets in the 1592 Korean expedition, and was made counsellor to Hideyoshi's nephew, Hidetoshi. Later, he fought in the critical battle of Sekigahara. Takatora's career typifies the spirit of the Momoyama warlord.

The domed bowl is made of five iron plates, and the exaggerated, sloping rabbit ears are of lacquered leather. In Japan, the hare is a symbol of longevity and was a favorite motif warriors used for their fanciful helmets.

19. Helmet in the form of a catfish tail
Early Edo period, early 17th century
Iron, black lacquer on *harikake*
Height: 37.1 cm.
Fukuoka City Museum, Fukuoka Prefecture

This helmet is part of a set of armor worn by the daimyo Kuroda Tadayuki (d. 1655) when, in 1637, at the order of the Edo shogunate he went to Shimabara on the island of Kyushu to suppress peasant uprisings led by Christian samurai.

Helmets shaped with rounded peaks are named for the tail of the catfish, *namazu*. Seen from the front, the abstract form has the sleek, economical beauty of an aircraft. The fish tail, lacquered black and probably made of leather, rests on an iron-plate bowl. The pointed projections represent its lateral fins. From the standpoint of both craftsmanship and art, this helmet, which is light for its size, is outstanding.

20. Helmet in the form of bracken-fern heads tied in a bundle

Early Edo period, early 17th century
Iron, silver leaf on lacquered *harikake*, black and red lacquer on wood
Height: 36.1 cm.
Collection of Takuji Yokota, Hiroshima Prefecture

From the sixteenth century, the military elite selected various objects from the world of nature to use for the adornment of helmets. While some images were chosen for their auspicious meaning, others had no other purpose than to distinguish the wearer with some outstanding form. In this fashion, this helmet employs a stylized version of a bundle of the edible bracken-fern heads that grow wild in the mountains and fields of Japan. The process of abstraction makes the heads of the ferns, called *warabi*, look like two great eyes when the helmet is viewed from the front. The bracken-fern heads and the cord binding them are of lacquered *harikake* covered with silver leaf and attached to a helmet bowl made of five iron plates. The plastic forms of the helmet are excellent; and the silver, oxidized to a dull black, has a calming influence on the beholder. The frontal ornament, carved in wood and lacquered, represents the horned mythical lion, a favorite talisman for the samurai.

21. Helmet with decorations in the form of two folded pieces of paper

Early Edo period, early 17th century
Iron
Height: 37.4 cm.
Collection of Tadao Nishiyama, Saitama Prefecture

The unusual decoration surmounting this fine helmet represents two square pieces of paper folded lightly on the diagonal. Resembling two flags, the exact meaning of this motif is unknown. It is possible that such sculptural fancy was simply intended to call attention to the wearer. The brim, in the shape of eyebrows, has been hammered out from the inner side of the dome.

22. Helmet in the form of a crouching rabbit
Early Edo period, early 17th century
Black lacquer on iron with silver leaf
Height: 18.5 cm.
Yamaguchi Kobunka Zaidan, Tokyo

The rabbit, whose associations are venerable, plays a part in many oriental legends. As an emblem of longevity, it was a favorite motif for samurai. In this helmet, a crouching rabbit has been hammered from sheets of iron. Its long ears serve as the major decorative element. The helmet has been lacquered black and covered in silver leaf, which over the years has oxidized and worn away.

23. Helmet decorated with yak hair
Early Edo period, early 17th century
Iron, yak hair
Height: 15.6 cm.
Collection of Tadao Nishiyama,
   Saitama Prefecture

Hair from yaks inhabiting the mountains of Yunan province, in China,
was imported to Japan from ancient
times for various kinds of ornament.
Rare and costly, yak hair was a
luxury item for the privileged classes. In
this helmet, a shock of long, loose yak hair
is attached to the central hole of an iron
helmet-bowl. It falls in ghostly dishevel-
ment about the fierce iron face mask.

24. Helmet bearing the face of the Buddhist deity Aizen Myō-ō, King of Passion
Edo period, 17th century
Iron, colored lacquer on wood, yak hair, glass
Height: 34.1 cm.
Collection of Keisuke Nakamiya, Osaka

Aizen Myō-ō, or Rāgarāja, is the deity in the Buddhist pantheon who purifies and enlightens the mind prone to obsession with physical passion. The brilliant red of his overpowering face symbolizes love and sexual desire. Myō-ō are prominent deities in Esoteric Buddhism, and their fierce poses and angry expressions indicate their power to overcome evil forces.

A wooden, vermilion-lacquered face of Rāgarāja is attached to the front of this iron helmet and is surmounted with a lion-head diadem topped with a mane of white yak hair, long a costly decorative material imported from the mountainous region of Yunan, China. In the tradition of Japanese Buddhist sculptural techniques, the deity's eyes are inset with glass.

25. Helmet in the form of a *yamabushi* priest's hat

Edo period, 17th century
Iron, wood
Height: 17.3 cm.
Collection of Shizue Yonetani, Kyoto

Believers in a religious practice called *shugendō*, a combination of primitive Japanese mountain worship and Buddhist asceticism, once traveled deep into mountainous regions to discipline themselves physically and spiritually. This helmet is patterned after the hat worn by such mountaineer-ascetics (*yamabushi*). The iron helmet-bowl is topped with a replica of the small hat, which is worn just above the forehead and tied at the chin with a cord. The twelve ribs of the hat represent the "twelvefold chain of causal origination" (*jūni-innen*), which, in Buddhist teaching, is the explanation for the causes of human happiness and unhappiness from the past, to the present, and into the future. A carving of a sutra scroll, representing Buddhist teachings, is attached to the front of the helmet. A rosary of 108 beads, which is used to eliminate the sufferings said to plague humankind, accompanies the helmet. In the face of the constant threat of death on the field of battle, warriors no doubt found spiritual support in religious symbolism of this kind.

27. Helmet in the form of the head of the God of Longevity
Edo period, 17th century
Iron, colored lacquer on *harikake*
Height: 24.5 cm.
Collection of Kiyotsugu Kurimoto, Hiroshima Prefecture

The long head of the God of Longevity, one of the popularly-worshiped Seven Gods of Good Fortune, was among the motifs taken from folklore for *kawari kabuto* designs (see cat. no. 8). In this version, the form of the elongated head is divided into bands, each finished in a different color and displaying a different technique of lacquer. The helmet thus demonstrates the sophisticated skills of lacquer workers of the Edo period. Ears are attached to the sides of the helmet, and brows have been worked into the brim.

28. Variation of the so-called bullet-shaped helmet

Early Edo period, 17th century
Iron, red lacquer on wood, gilt metal
Height: 26.5 cm.
Collection of Sei'ichi Asano, Tokyo

Western armor was introduced into Japan in the mid-sixteenth century with the establishment of official contact between the Europeans and Japanese. Leading daimyo expressed their enthusiasm for the exotic culture of the "Southern barbarians" by adoptating Western armor. While some morion and cabasset helmets were actually used by the Japanese, more often Japanese armorers copied and adapted their own styles. These are known as *hōdan* or bullet-shaped helmets because of their resemblance in form to the European bullet and cannonball. By the seventeenth century, such helmets had become popular.

This helmet, part of a suit of armor that belonged to Matsudaira Yasuchika (d.1618), a daimyo of the illustrious Matsudaira clan of Echizen (modern Fukui Prefecture), represents the attempts of a local armorer to assimilate Western styles and adjust them to Japanese tastes.

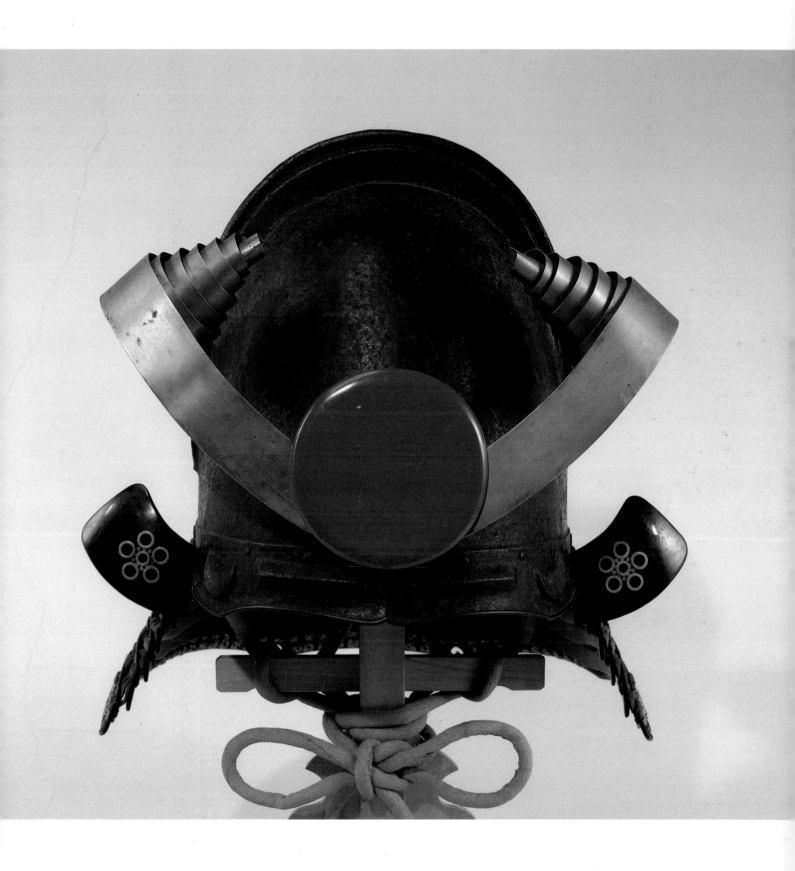

29. Helmet with holly-leaf ornament
Edo period, 17th century
Iron, lacquer on *harikake*, wild boar
  and bear hair
Height: 19.0 cm.
Collection of Tadamasa Mitsuhashi, Tokyo

Aside from the oversized frontal ornament representing holly leaves (*hiiragi*), talismatic in Japan, this helmet is outstanding for its covering of bear and wild boar hair that is arranged in an unbound hair-style of a full-grown young man of the period. The sight of a warrior riding into battle with what looks like a bared head certainly would have startled the enemy.

30. Helmet in the form of a courtier's hat
Edo period, 17th century
Iron, black and yellow lacquer on *harikake*
Height: 39.3 cm.
Collection of Takuji Yokota, Hiroshima Prefecture

This helmet, rising from a four-plated iron bowl, is fashioned after the long hat, called *naga-eboshi*, one of several variations of the *eboshi*, the traditional headgear of Japanese aristocrats and warriors. Helmets in this form were popular in the sixteenth century. This one is finished in a tortoise-shell pattern rendered in black and yellow lacquer.

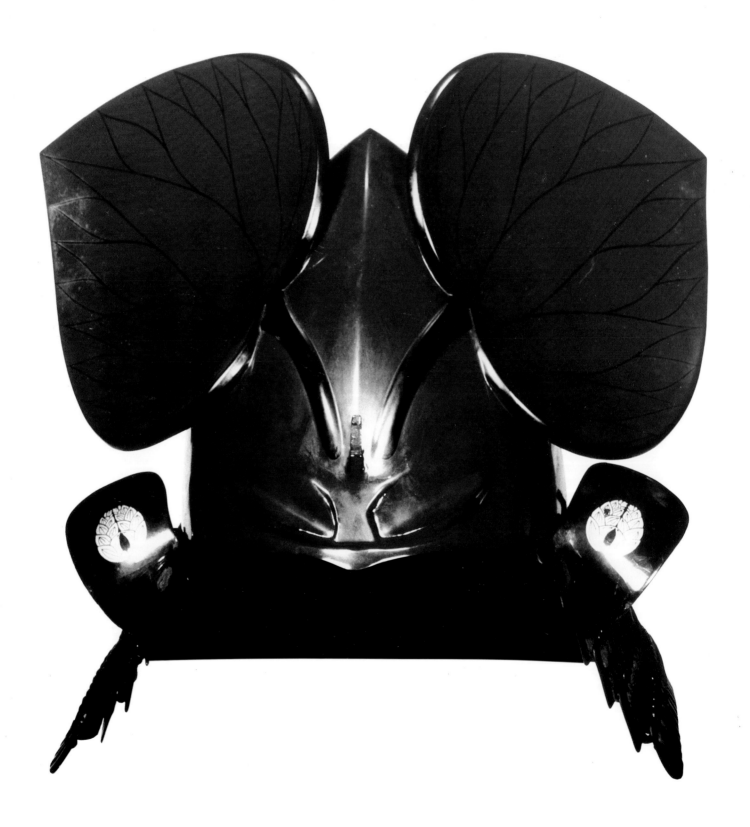

31. Helmet with hollyhock leaves
Edo period, 17th century
Iron, lacquer on *harikake*
Height: 23.0 cm.
National Museum of Japanese History, Chiba Prefecture

The leaf of the Japanese hollyhock (*aoi*) has long been a popular design motif and figures in the crest of the house of Tokugawa, shoguns from the early seventeenth to the middle of the nineteenth century. On either side of this pointed iron helmet is a hollyhock leaf in lacquered *harikake*. Most of the helmet is finished in a brownish-black lacquer, produced by mixing ferric hydroxide powder with black lacquer. The stems, veins, and outlines of the leaves, however, are lacquered black. This helmet, pleasing and powerful in form, demonstrates outstanding craftsmanship.

32. Helmet in the form of a bear's head
Edo period, 17th century
Iron, gold and red lacquer on *harikake*, bear hair
Height: 32.5 cm.
Collection of Takuji Yokota, Hiroshima Prefecture

The bear is regarded as "the king of beasts" in Japan for its strength and ferocity, and the use of its head to surmount this helmet was certainly intended to awaken fear, and to make the wearer highly conspicuous. Animals are often used as motifs for *kawari kabuto*, but this degree of realistic depiction is rare.

The bear's head is constructed of lacquered *harikake* covered with actual bear hair. The eyes are painted in gold, and the ears are exaggerated in size to enhance the helmet's overall design. The craftsmanship of this bold and unusual piece is quite remarkable.

33. Helmet surmounted with a butterfly
Edo period, 17th century
Iron, black lacquer on *harikake*
Height: 38.8 cm.
Collection of Takuji Yokota, Hiroshima Prefecture

Because of its elegance and beauty, the butterfly was a cherished design motif in Japan for centuries. In this instance, a butterfly form in lacquered *harikake* is sculpted on the top of an iron helmet-bowl. But the abstract treatment makes the form susceptible to different interpretations. This helmet illustrates how the aesthetic approach of Japanese warriors some three hundred years ago is astonishingly close to the modern.

34. Catfish-tail helmet adorned with peacock feathers and yak hair

Edo period, 17th century
Iron, *harikake*, peacock feathers, yak hair, gilt metal
Height: 52.0 cm.
Takatsu Kobunka Kaikan, Kyoto

The late sixteenth century in Japan saw the opening of official trade with Europe, and the elements of Western culture that were imported at that time stimulated a craze for the exotic and foreign. *Kawari kabuto* were often designed in response to the new fashion, popular among the leading daimyo, and incorporated materials that were altogether foreign to Japan. In this helmet, peacock tail feathers cover the entire rise of the helmet form, which is made of *harikake* in the so-called catfish-tail shape. The plumes, probably obtained as a result of trade with Europe or China, were no doubt costly, as was the Chinese yak hair.

This helmet was part of a suit of armor belonging to the Mōri family, once daimyo in what is now Yamaguchi Prefecture.

35. Helmet in the form of a fish tail
Edo period, 17th century
Iron, silver leaf on lacquered *harikake*
Height: 28.4 cm.
Takatsu Kobunka Kaikan, Kyoto

The representation of a fish tail executed in *harikake* and covered in silver leaf tops a bullet-shaped helmet-bowl composed of iron plates, the tilted caudal fin forming the pinnacle. The lateral ornaments are the shape of pectoral fins, though they resemble mammalian ears. The designer's skill is evident in the way he has stylized the fish form without effacing it. The neck-guard is composed of long, thin iron plates lacquered brownish-black and connected by textured leather thongs.

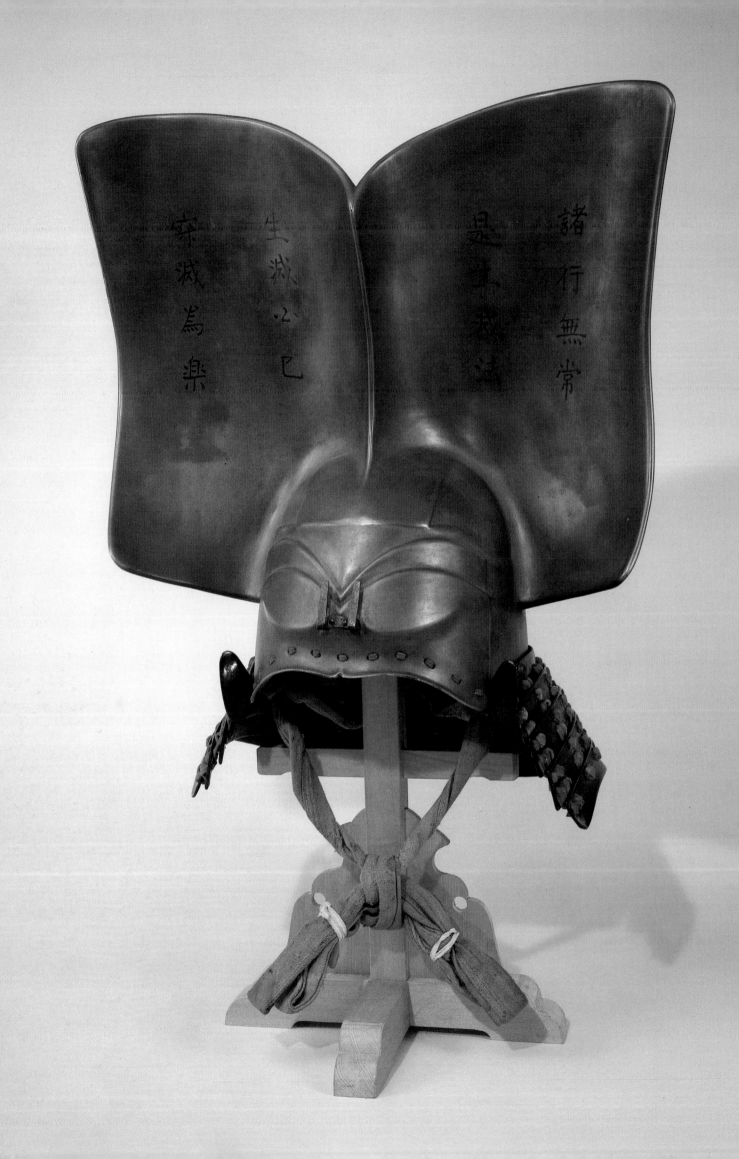

36. Helmet in the shape of Ichi-no-tani Canyon, inscribed with a Buddhist quatrain

Edo period, 17th century
Iron, *gindami* on *harikake*
Height: 41.8 cm.
Collection of Tadao Nishiyama, Saitama Prefecture

This helmet is another example of those representing the precipitous walls of the valley known as Ichi-no-tani, where the celebrated warrior Minamoto Yoritomo defeated the Taira clan in 1184. (See cat. nos. 9 and 26.) Here, the decorative part of the helmet is formed of lacquer on *harikake* and set on a domed bowl composed of three iron plates. Though simple, the form is sculpturesque and modern in feeling. It is finished in the *gindami* lacquer technique, whereby silver dust is sprinkled on a wet coat of clear lacquer.

The inscription on the helmet is a well-known quote from a Buddhist text. It reads:

> All is vanity and evanescence.
> That is the law of life and death.
> In the complete denial of life and death
> Is the bliss of entering Nirvana.

This quatrain is associated with the opening verse of *The Tale of the Heike*, the epic tale that recounts the fall of the Taira clan in the twelfth century.

37. Helmet in the form of a conch-shell trumpet

Edo period, 17th century
Iron inlaid with silver and gold, lacquer coating
Height: 22.2 cm.
Collection of Kiyotsugu Kurimoto, Hiroshima Prefecture

From ancient times, trumpets made of conch shells drawn from nearby seas or from the South Seas have been employed in Buddhist ceremonies, and on the battlefield for the sounding of battle signals. Among warriors, the shell itself was prized and used only by leaders.

It took an armorer of great skill to hammer the complicated form of this helmet from a single sheet of iron. The piece is decorated with inlays of gold and silver and coated with a thin layer of lacquer for protection. While full lacquer treatment enhances the beauty of the helmet and protects it from moisture and rusting, it also hides the metal work. When the tempering and metal work have been especially skillful, this can be undesirable. Exposing the iron entirely to the atmosphere, however, does invite rusting and so, with fine iron helmets such as this one, a thin coat of transparent lacquer is applied to the surface.

39. Helmet in the form of a sheaf of *yuzuriha* leaves

Edo period, 17th century
Iron, silver leaf on lacquered *harikake*
Height: 22.9 cm.
Collection of Keisuke Nakamiya, Osaka

When the new leaves appear on the plant called *yuzuriha*—which grows wild from the central part of Japan to Korea—the old leaves drop to make way for them. Since this may be interpreted as a symbol of the peaceful succession of one generation of a family by another, the Japanese have long considered this plant auspicious. In this helmet, twelve of these leaves made of black-lacquered *harikake* covered in silver leaf and bound together at the pinnacle, are set on top of an iron helmet-bowl. The unusual shape of this motif, its auspicious connotations, and its refined craftsmanship make it altogether typical of the *kawari kabuto* genre.

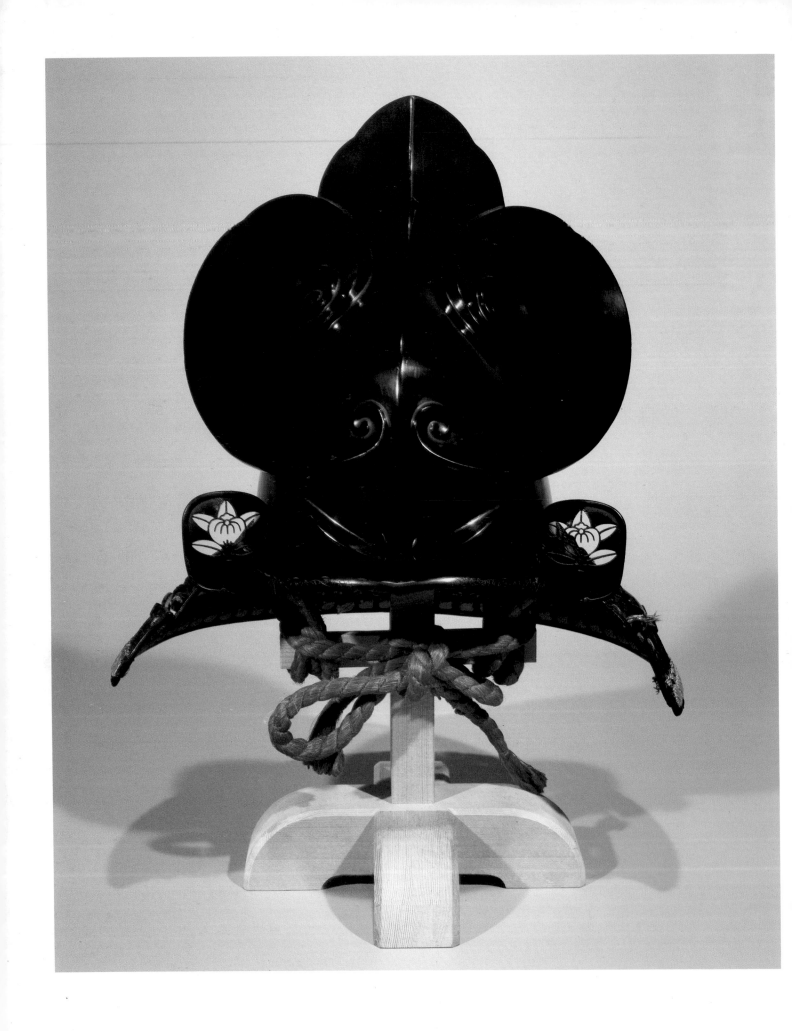

112

40. Helmet in the form of hollyhock leaves
Edo period, 17th century
Iron, black lacquer on *harikake*
Height: 29.3 cm.
Collection of Tadao Yoshii, Osaka

The leaves of the ornamental hollyhock (*aoi*) appear in the crest of the Tokugawa family, Japan's ruling shogunate from the seventeenth to the middle of the nineteenth century. In this instance, the leaves have been so stylized that they evoke other associations. The domed helmet-bowl, composed of five iron plates, is surmounted by the curvilinear hollyhock-leaf ornament, which is made of black-lacquered *harikake*.

41. Helmet in the form of *kashiwa* oak leaves

Edo period, 17th century
Iron, black lacquer on *harikake*, gilt metal
Height: 38.7 cm.
Takatsu Kobunka Kaikan, Kyoto

Shinto gods are believed to reside in the great *kashiwa* oak tree, and in Shinto ceremonies, the *kashiwa* leaves are often placed on the platters of food offered to those divinities. Two leaves joined together form the composition of this helmet, which is made of black-lacquered *harikake* surmounting an iron bowl. From the front, the helmet resembles an *eboshi*, the traditional courtier's hat, but the side view reveals a fairly realistic representation of the leaves. A gilt-metal ornament in the shape of a radially-arranged bamboo leaf crowns the front, while crests with the *kashiwa* oak are embossed on the helmet's brim. This helmet is an outstanding example of a *kawari kabuto* devoted to plant forms, a favorite and often auspicious motif for the military elite of Japan.

42. Helmet in the form of an inverted bowl
Edo period, 17th century
Red lacquer on iron
Height: 19.0 cm.
Fukuoka City Museum, Fukuoka Prefecture

This remarkable helmet is in the shape of an ordinary food bowl, enlarged and inverted on the head. The type of bowl this is fashioned after comes with a lid and is called a *gōsu*. The choice of such a form, which has no direct auspicious or symbolic meaning, is startling.

An inscription records that this helmet was commissioned in 1688 by the grandchildren of the Kyushu daimyo, Kuroda Toshitaka (1546–1604), as a copy of one he had worn. (This helmet is now in the collection of the Morioka Kyōdo Shriryō-kan.) Using the original, which was covered in silver leaf, two families of armorers —Haruta and Iwai—were commissioned to create this helmet.

43. Helmet in the form of a Southern-barbarian hat
Edo period, 17th century
Iron and silver
Height: 22.0 cm.
Nishimura Museum, Yamaguchi Prefecture

Southern barbarians was the term the Japanese used to describe Europeans who came into their country, by a southern route, in the sixteenth century. These visitors—traders and missionaries from Portugal, Spain, and the Netherlands, for the most part—wore cloaks and felt hats and other curious fashion that the Japanese fancied, much as they did European armor. Indeed, the arrival of the Europeans inspired something of a boom for the exotic and foreign, and the cultural epoch spanning the mid-sixteenth to mid-seventeenth century is marked by a degree of Western influence. This iron helmet, decorated with European design patterns expressed in a Japanese manner, is in the shape of a kind of Western felt hat. The warrior who wore it must have been in the very vanguard of fashion for his time.

44. Morning-glory helmet
Edo period, 17th century
Iron, gilt metal
Height: 36.6 cm.
Collection of Tadamasa Mitsuhashi, Tokyo

This helmet in the graceful, flaring form of a morning glory blossom is composed of eleven iron plates. Inscribed on the inner surfaces of the petals are the names of twelve gods, on whose assistance a warrior about to face possible death in battle might wish to call. An engraved cipher records that the armor was made by Myōchin Nobuie, who lived in Iwaki (in modern Fukushima Prefecture). Nobuie was a famous armorer active from the sixteenth century into the seventeenth century. The elegant form, which recalls the shape of Mount Fuji, is unexpected for a helmet.

45. Helmet adorned with sutra scrolls
Edo period, 17th century
Iron, black lacquer on *harikake*
Height: 30.1 cm.
Collection of Kiyotsugu Kurimoto, Hiroshima Prefecture

On the battlefield, the Japanese warrior came face to face with death. In the name of justice, he was called upon to battle against, possibly kill, and risk his own life in facing, others against whom he felt no personal hostility. Desiring protection, he often sought faith in the Buddha. The simplest expression of this was to inscribe the name of a Buddhist deity on his helmet, or to insert an amulet somewhere in the headgear. The use of emblems such as these two sutra scrolls, representing the Buddhist doctrine, as ornaments for the battle crown symbolizes the warrior's traditional desire to assimilate Buddhist teachings in his approach to life and death, but in new form. The religious image here dominates the entire design of the helmet. This striking composition, probably made of leather, is an extraordinary example of *kawari kabuto*.

46. Helmet adorned with a dragonfly
Edo period, 17th century
Iron, gold and black lacquer on wood, gilt metal
Height: 26.0 cm.
Nishimura Museum, Yamaguchi Prefecture

The dragonfly, traditionally known as *katsumushi* or the "invincible insect," was a favorite symbol of strength among Japanese warriors. A gold-lacquered dragonfly, with its wings and body detailed in black and red lacquer, is the frontal ornament of this dome-shaped helmet. Composed of three iron plates, the helmet is surmounted with a bent iron plate of abstract form, whose exact meaning is obscure. It might suggest a hat, a butterfly, a mollusk, a mountain, a fish tail, or any number of forms. The exceptional iron work has been left revealed, uncoated. The rear ornament consists of five radially-arranged leaves of the plant called *barin*, of the hemp family. This halo of golden rays lends majesty and fancy to this fine helmet.

47. Helmet with an abstract form
Edo period, 17th century
Black-lacquered iron
Height: 21.7 cm.
Collection of Kiyotsugu Kurimoto, Hiroshima Prefecture

This helmet is said to have belonged to Tokugawa Ieyasu (1542-1616), founder of the Tokugawa shogunate. Ieyasu was the brilliant military leader who completed the drive of national unification, begun in the late sixteenth century by Oda Nobunaga and Toyotomi Hideyoshi, and who, from 1615 with the Battle of Osaka Castle, established the unchallenged rule of the Tokugawa house which was to last until 1868.

The central part of this carefully executed helmet is a bullet-form consisting of seven iron plates. On both sides are curvilinear forms of indefinite meaning. The entire helmet is heavily finished in black lacquer. Though the image is not identifiable, perhaps antique Chinese headgear was the source for its shape.

48. Helmet in the form of a lobster tail

Early Edo period, 17th century
Iron, black lacquer on leather
Height: 49.5 cm.
Yamaguchi Kobunka Zaidan, Tokyo

A lobster tail executed in leather and lacquered black surmounts a domed helmet-bowl consisting of five iron plates. To warriors, the lobster was symbolic. With its articulated carapace, the animal is, like the samurai, armored. The lobster is as well a traditional emblem of longevity, and is thus an auspicious motif for the helmet. The upward dash of the tail suggests courage.

49. Helmet in the odd form of a stack of rings
Edo period, 17th century
Iron, black lacquer on *harikake*
Height: 35.0 cm.
National Museum of Japanese History, Chiba Prefecture

The daimyo of the sixteenth and seventeenth centuries who commissioned helmets, whether for battle or for parade, demanded of the armorers a headpiece that would exert a personal image of power, a distinct charisma. At times, whimsy alone dictated the forms for *kawari kabuto*. The precise meaning of some helmet shapes —such as this one which is described as *wagasane igyō* or "odd form of a stack of rings"—is thus uncertain.

50. Helmet in the form of a cloth hood
Edo period, 17th century
Iron, black lacquer on *harikake*, silver leaf on wood
Height: 19.6 cm.
Collection of Takuji Yokota, Hiroshima Prefecture

Hoods were a favorite shape warriors sculpted on top of their helmets, though the reasons for this liking are not clear. On top of this slightly pointed helmet-bowl, which consists of six iron plates, the front end of a folded cloth hood (*zukin*), turned forward in a double layer, has been rendered in *harikake* and lacquered black. The knot of the head-band forms the frontal ornament.

51. Helmet in the form of a *nage-zukin* cloth hood
Edo period, 17th century
Iron, black lacquer on *harikake*, gold leaf on wood
Height: 16.3 cm.
Collection of Takuji Yokota, Hiroshima Prefecture

A *nage-zukin* hood is one in which the pointed fold is turned back towards the rear. In this helmet, a *nage-zukin* form is constructed in *harikake* and set upon a slightly pointed, iron helmet-bowl. The knot of the headband has been carved of wood and finished in gold leaf. Contemporary accounts record that this style of helmet was in vogue among military commanders.

52. Pumpkin-shaped helmet
Edo period, 17th century
Iron, silver leaf on lacquered *harikake*
Height: 17.2 cm.
Collection of Kiyotsugu Kurimoto, Hiroshima Prefecture

During the seventeenth century, the pumpkin was imported into Japan from Cambodia and was consequently given the Japanese appellation of *kabocha*. Unusual when it initially appeared, it was just the sort of motif warlords who celebrated novel and exotic fashion would have fancied — whether for parades, for the battlefield, or for stage.

Composed of eight iron plates, this helmet-bowl is surmounted with a *harikake* pumpkin that is lacquered black and finished in silver leaf.

56. Helmet in the form of a Buddhist bell
Edo period, 18th century
Iron, gilt metal
Height: 30.0 cm.
Yamaguchi Kobunka Zaidan, Tokyo

This helmet is in the shape of a *bonshō*, the large bronze Buddhist bells which hang in the pavilions of Buddhist temples and are struck to mark the hours or to signify the carrying out of religious ceremonies. This piece is an excellent example of the great skill with which Edo-period armorers could hammer various shapes from single sheets of iron. The frontal ornament is a pole of the kind used to strike these bells (they do not have internal clappers). It is surmounted by a weapon in the form of a rake.

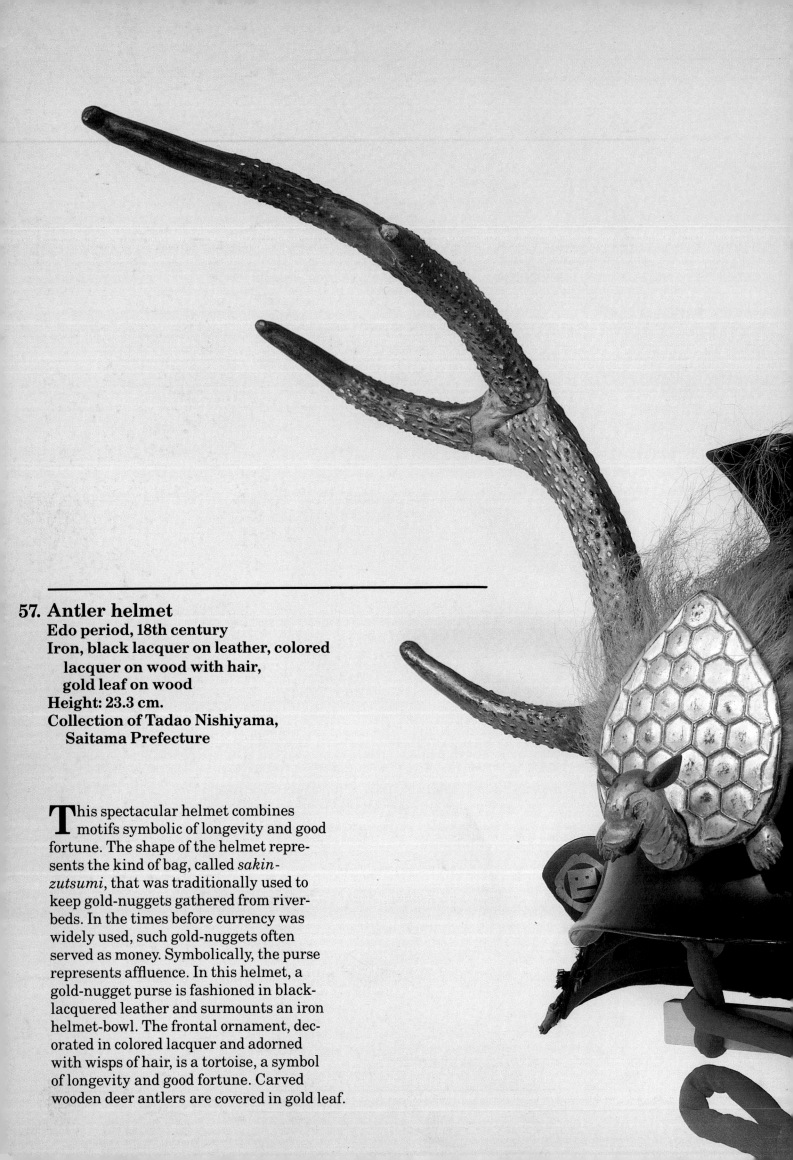

57. Antler helmet
Edo period, 18th century
Iron, black lacquer on leather, colored
   lacquer on wood with hair,
   gold leaf on wood
Height: 23.3 cm.
Collection of Tadao Nishiyama,
   Saitama Prefecture

This spectacular helmet combines
motifs symbolic of longevity and good
fortune. The shape of the helmet represents the kind of bag, called *sakin-
zutsumi*, that was traditionally used to
keep gold-nuggets gathered from river-
beds. In the times before currency was
widely used, such gold-nuggets often
served as money. Symbolically, the purse
represents affluence. In this helmet, a
gold-nugget purse is fashioned in black-
lacquered leather and surmounts an iron
helmet-bowl. The frontal ornament, decorated in colored lacquer and adorned
with wisps of hair, is a tortoise, a symbol
of longevity and good fortune. Carved
wooden deer antlers are covered in gold leaf.

58. Helmet with a *gumbai* fan
Edo period, 18th century
Iron
Height: 21.0 cm.
Collection of Motoyuki Shiroaya, Hyōgo Prefecture

This fine iron helmet, which has been left un-lacquered to reveal the metal work, displays on its front the kind of butterfly-shaped fan that was used by military commanders for giving orders on the battlefield. Contemporary screen paintings of famous battles of the sixteenth and early seventeenth centuries depict the use of such fans, called *gumbai*. This helmet, made during the age of "Great Peace," was probably commissioned by a high-ranking samurai.

59. Helmet decorated with crab claws
Edo period, 18th century
Iron, black lacquer on *harikake*, gold leaf on wood
Height: 19.5 cm.
Nishimura Museum, Yamaguchi Prefecture

The crab was a favorite symbol for the samurai, and appears as a design motif in sword guards and stirrups as well as in *kawari kabuto*. Like the lobster and the clam shell, the crab's appealed to the warrior as an emblem of his own self-defense. The crab's claws, which are used to seize and mangle other creatures, attached in this way to a helmet were no doubt intended to inspire awe.

60. Eggplant helmet
Edo period, 18th century
Iron
Height: 23.0 cm.
Ana Hachiman Shrine, Tokyo

Fruits and vegetables were typically the inspiration for *kawari kabuto* forms, some because they were auspicious, some because they were foreign and exotic, and some for no reason at all save for show. Persimmons, pomegrants, acorns, gourds, and pumpkins (see cat. no. 52) are among those found on helmets of the period.

This helmet is sculpted as the stem of an eggplant. Native to India, the eggplant has long been cultivated and cooked in a variety of ways in Japan, but it hasn't any specific meaning. The ability to hammer such a form from a single sheet of iron, at a time before the invention of pressing machinery, indicates the very high level of metal craftsmanship available in Japan in the Edo period. Indeed, this was a time when armorers vied with each other in technical skill and, fully aware of the nature of the metal, were able to hammer difficult and unusual forms from iron.

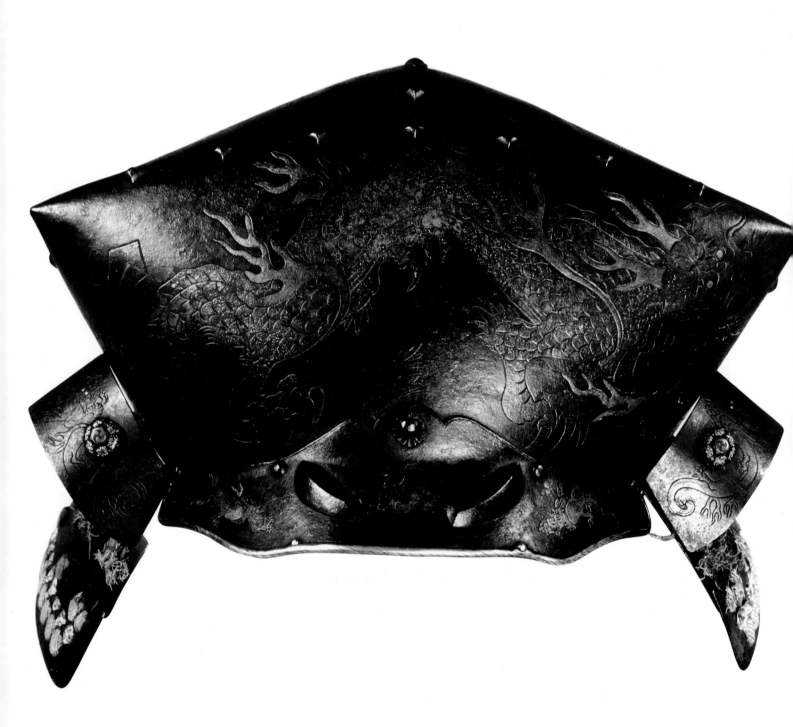

61. Helmet in the form of a woven-straw bag for grain
Edo period, 18th century
Iron inlaid with gold and silver
Height: 17.0 cm.
Collection of Hajime Fujita, Okayama Prefecture

Characteristic of *kawari kabuto* is the willingness and delight of the military elite to crown their heads at the most serious occasions of ceremony and duty with sculptures of lowly, ordinary articles. In this example, a woven-straw bag used for storing grain has been transformed into a spectacular helmet, a samurai's identification.

The helmet is made of two sheets of iron inlaid front and back in silver and gold. A dragon adorns the front, and *sayagata* key-fret patterns adorn the rear. The name of the armorer, Fujiwara Yoichi, is engraved on the inner surface.

156

62. Helmet with eyeglasses
Edo period, 18th century
Iron, gold leaf on wood
Height: 20.8 cm.
National Museum of Japanese History,
   Chiba Prefecture

Eyeglasses were first used in Japan in the early seventeenth century or so, but this is the only known example of their being applied to a helmet. Introduced by the Southern barbarians —the Japanese appelation for visitors from Europe—eyeglasses caused a sensation among the status- and fashion-conscious military elite. Added to this exotic fancy are feather-like wings on either side of the helmet. These represent the plumage of Tengu, the Japanese mountain goblin with a face of a human, a long nose, wings, and magical powers.

Eight iron plates create the pointed acorn- or bullet-shaped helmet-bowl, derived from European prototypes. The metal has been left un-lacquered to reveal the fine quality of the iron work.

63. Helmet with dancing dragon motif
Edo period, 18th century
Iron, lacquer coating
Height: 25.2 cm.
National Museum of Japanese History, Chiba Prefecture

The front of this helmet is shaped after the graceful curves that represent the dragon dancing in the traditional arabesque-like pattern called the *karakusa-ryūmon*, common in Japanese metal, textile, and decorative arts. The central part of the helmet, which is made of eight iron plates, is pointed; at the front, a tricorn-like iron plate is attached. The brim sweeps upward, complementing the sloping, curvilinear composition of the upper body. The excellent metal work has been left un-lacquered, a technique known as *kanasabi-ji*.

64. Helmet with hollyhock-leaf crest
Edo period, 18th century
Iron
Height: 18.3 cm.
Collection of Yoshiaki Yoshida, Saitama Prefecture

Represented in the crest of the Kamo Shrine in Kyoto, one of the more important Shinto shrines, the hollyhock has long been considered an auspicious design motif. Its authority was greatly increased when it was adopted for the crest of the Tokugawa shogunal family, rulers of Japan from 1600 until 1868, and for all its collateral lines. This helmet, a literal representation of the family crest, was commissioned by a daimyo of the shogunal house.

This so-called acorn-shaped helmet is hammered from a single sheet of iron. The surface is divided into three panels, each of which is ornamented with an embossed hollyhock leaf, forming a complete three-dimensional crest. The same crest decorates the base of the helmet-bowl, while the brim displays an embossed dragon. Helmets usually incorporated the wearer's family crest somewhere in the design—usually on the earflaps, called *fukigaeshi*—but rarely was a design given over to its actual representation. The elaborate decoration of the helmet demonstrates the high level of metal craftsmanship of the Edo period.

65. Helmet with seashell and mythical lion
Edo period, 18th century
Iron, colored lacquer on wood
Height: 15.5 cm.
Yamaguchi Kobunka Zaidan, Tokyo

A large seashell caps this iron helmet, which is fronted with a horned mythical lion, the *shishi*. The shell, of the mollusk called *itaya-gai* found in Japanese coastal waters, was popular as a design motif because its shape resembles an opened fan, a symbol of celebration and happiness. Ridges simulating wrinkles in the human forehead are hammered in the brim, along with expressive eyebrows. The work on this helmet demonstrates the very highest level of Edo-period metal arts.

66. Helmet in the form of a boy's topknot
Edo period, 18th century
Iron, black lacquer on *harikake*, gold leaf, bear hair
Height: 26.3 cm.
Collection of Takuji Yokota, Hiroshima Prefecture

From the twelfth to the sixteenth century in Japan, boys of the upper class wore their hair bound on top of their heads in two rings, like those in the black-lacquered *harikake* ornament surmounting the pointed bowl of this helmet.

The ring of the helmet is covered with bear hair, to suggest the actual hairline of a young boy's forehead. Embossed eyebrows covered with gold leaf accentuate the brim. The realism expressed in helmets such as this one reflects a style common in helmets of this period.

67. Helmet in the form of a head covering
Edo period, 18th century
Iron, *harikake*, white wool
Height: 20.7 cm.
Collection of Kiyotsugu Kurimoto, Hiroshima Prefecture

Traditional head coverings made of tied or folded cloth were often the inspiration for *kawari kabuto* shapes. (See cat. nos. 6 and 13.) This helmet, based on a *makkō* head covering that was worn to protect the coiffure or to tie one's hair back when engaged in work, is unusual in that it is covered with white woolen fabric imported from Europe.

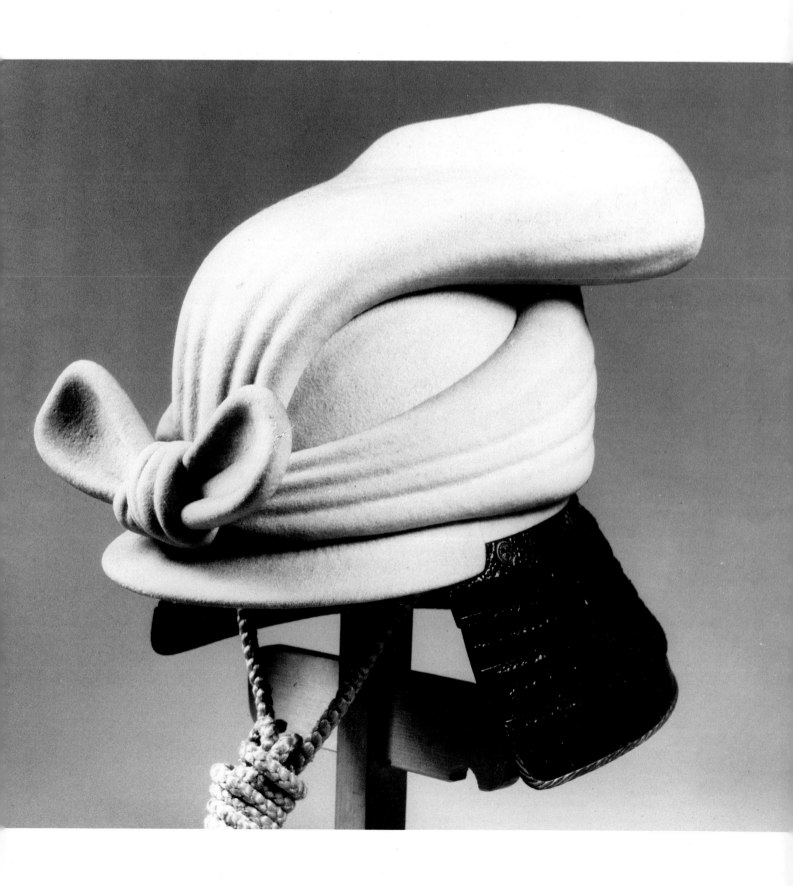

68. Pointed-crown helmet with abalone ornaments

Edo period, 19th century
Iron, black lacquer and gold *maki-e* on wood
Height: 21.5 cm.
Takatsu Kobunka Kaikan, Kyoto

European armor was introduced to Japan in the mid-sixteenth century with the arrival of the Portuguese traders. Like other aspects of Western fashion, it caused a sensation among the leading daimyo who, in their rivalry for local advantage, were eager to assimilate new technology for their armor. The cabasset and morion helmet types appealed greatly to the warlords, and it is known that certain of them actually wore some—often backward, so that the rear hole for plumage could hold the frontal ornament so essential to Japanese helmet design. More often, however, the European technique of manufacture and their pointed-crown forms were copied and adapted by armorers in Japan. The Japanese typically adorned such helmets with decorative motifs derived from their own folklore, and with traditional neck-guards.

The basic shape of this helmet is an example of the European-inspired *kabuto*. Cutout patterns resembling Western ornamentation adorn the rim, and, in the spirit of European helmets, the iron has been left un-lacquered. Two abolone shells carved in wood, lacquered black and highlighted with gold *maki-e*, are attached to the helmet. The abalone is an auspicious emblem in Japan for longevity and was favored by the military elite. The helmet is inscribed and records that is was made by armorers Iwai Sadakichi and Sadamiki, in 1819.

69. Naruto whirlpool helmet
Edo period, 18th century
Iron
Height: 28.0 cm.
Collection of Tadamasa Mitsuhashi, Tokyo

Composed of four thin sheets of iron, this helmet is fashioned to suggest the Naruto whirlpools that roar in a strait in the Seto Inland Sea when the water flows violently at low tide. Natural phenomena—waves, flames, great mountains—were often abstracted for the helmet design, and danger zones such as whirlpools were also favored. (See cat. no. 11.)

Hammered from thin iron, this unusual piece demanded great technical skill. Its towering form would have been impressive in the kind of parade for which helmets of this period were typically made.

171

70. Mountain valley helmet
Edo period, 18th century
Gold leaf on lacquered *harikake*
Height: 27.4 cm.
Takatsu Kobunka Kaikan, Kyoto

This spectacular helmet is the only surviving example of an all paper *kabuto*. While most *harikake* constructions of paper or leather surmount helmet-bowls made of iron that serve as the actual protection, this helmet is made entirely of laminated Japanese paper. Its form represents a valley between two peaks. It is impossible to say whether this particular one was intended for actual use, but written records do contain mention of warriors who fought in paper armor. Japanese paper, which is made of wood fiber, does not tear readily and, when laminated in several layers, is fairly strong. This helmet is heavily lacquered and covered in gold leaf.

72. Helmet in the form of a stylized orc
Edo period, 18th century
Iron, black lacquer with gold and silver paint on *harikake*, and brass
Height: 47.4 cm.
Takatsu Kobunka Kaikan, Kyoto

The orc, or killer whale, has long been associated in Japan with fantastic courage and ferocity. It was also an emblem of fire protection because it spouts water, and unglazed ceramic representations of the orc were often placed at the ends of castle roof ridges as a talisman against fire. Adopted by the military elite, who admired the valor suggested by its fierce face and sweeping tail, the orc often adorned their helmets.

Surmounting a pointed helmet-bowl composed of twelve iron plates is the *harikake* orc. The face is coated in lacquer textured by being tapped while still wet with a cloth-covered ball of cotton. The scales are lined in gold, and all the fins are removable. Brass sheets filigreed into wave patterns are set on either side of the body to suggest the ocean through which the creature swims.

In the sixteenth and early seventeenth centuries, helmet forms were simpler and more abstract. In the eighteenth century, when a strict central authority controlled an unchallenged peace and the military aristocracy had only material glory with which to prove their valor, greater stress was put on the *kabuto* ornamentation. Daimyo wore their helmets chiefly for parade and ceremony, and the need for protection was symbolic only. This helmet is an excellent example of the kind of elaborately decorative works which armorers vied to produce in this period.

73. Chain-mail helmet with centipede
Edo period, 18th century
Iron and iron chain mail, gilt metal
Height: 16.5 cm.
National Museum of Japanese History,
   Chiba Prefecture

Construction of chain mail was introduced from Europe in the sixteenth century along with other kinds of armor, and is called *namban-gusari* after the Southern barbarians. It was not customarily used for helmets and its use here is therefore unusual. The poisonous centipede, which figures in Japanese folklore, rises with magnificent menace across the front of this helmet.

74. Butterfly helmet
Edo period, 18th century
Iron, gold leaf
Height: 26.5 cm.
National Museum of Japanese History,
Chiba Prefecture

A butterfly made of iron is attached to a peach-form helmet-bowl composed of six iron plates. A white and gold butterfly, upside down, adorns this form. Cloud patterns are embossed on the brim and flaps of the helmet. The neck-guard is highly refined work of tooled and gilded leather.

This magnificent helmet is probably the work of armorers in Kaga (modern Ishikawa Prefecture), an area that was controlled by the illustrious Maeda daimyo.

75. Helmet with water-buffalo horns
Edo period, 19th century
Black lacquer on iron, gold leaf on lacquered wood
Height: 23.9 cm.
Fukuoka City Museum, Fukuoka Prefecture

The so-called peach-form is a Japanese version of a European helmet shape that was introduced in the sixteenth century and used considerably thereafter. Protruding from the elegant form are two sweeping horns, splendid and beautifully balanced representations of the handsome horns of the water buffalo of southern Asia. Carved in wood, they are lacquered black and covered in gold leaf. This helmet was commissioned by the Kyushu daimyo Kuroda Nagatomo as a copy of a helmet worn by his predecessor, the valient Momoyama warlord, Kuroda Nagamasa (1568–1623).

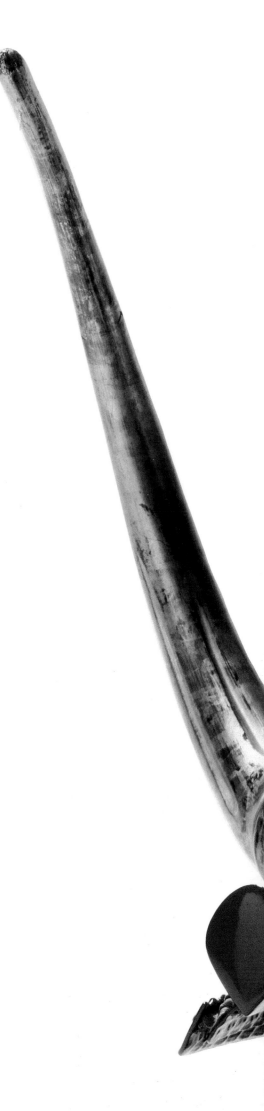

76. Helmet in the shape of a Southern-barbarian hat
Edo Period, 17th century
Iron
Height: 24.3 cm.
Collection of Tadao Nishiyama, Saitama Prefecture

The Japanese took a great fancy to the tall felt hats worn by the Europeans who came to Japan in the sixteenth century. These, along with other fashion and luxury accessories, caused a *namban* craze which lasted, if only covertly, well after the government's policy of seclusion had been established.

This helmet is a fairly realistic version of a European-style hat. The cutout metal patterns are Japanese copies of Western designs and are intended to produce an exotic effect. This unusual helmet is valuable as historical evidence of the influence European culture exerted upon Japanese armor.

CHRONOLOGY

Japanese Historical Periods

Jōmon	ca. 8000–300 B.C.
Yayoi	ca. 300 B.C.–A.D. 300
Kofun	ca. 300–552
Asuka	552–710
Nara	710–794
Early Heian	794–858
Late Heian (Fujiwara)	858–1185
Kamakura	1185–1333
Namboku-cho	1333–1336
Muromachi (Ashikaga)	1336–1573
Azuchi-Momoyama	1573–1600
Tokugawa (Edo)	1600–1868
Meiji	1868–1912
Meiji-present	1912–

Outstanding Political Events
of the Sengoku, Momoyama and Early Edo Periods

1467–1477	Ōnin War. Sengoku era, the period of "the country at war," begins.
1500	Civil strife throughout Japan. Fragmentation of central authority and rise of provincial warlord daimyo.
1543	Portuguese trading ship arrives at Tanegashima, off the coast of Kyushu. Firearms introduced.
1549	Francis Xavier (1507–52) reaches Japan. Christianity introduced.
1568	Oda Nobunaga (1534–82) leads drive toward national unification and occupies the imperial capital of Kyoto.
1571	Nobunaga demolishes Hiei-san monasteries and wages war on the Buddhist church.
1573	End of Muromachi shogunate. Nobunaga forces shogun Ashikaga Yoshiake out of Kyoto and assumes the position of shogun.
1575	Battle of Nagashino. Firearms used for the first time.
1576	Construction of Nobunaga's Azuchi castle. Cannon introduced.
1577	Toyotomi Hideyoshi (1536–98) leads Nobunaga's campaign against daimyo in western Japan.
1582	Nobunaga assassinated by Akechi Mitsuhide. Hideyoshi succeeds him as military leader in drive toward unification.
1584	Battle of Nagakute.
1585	Hideyoshi appointed chief advisor to the throne.
1586	Hideyoshi builds Osaka castle and is appointed Prime Minister.
1587	First Christian persecution. Hideyoshi's grand open-invitation tea ceremony at Kitano in Kyoto.
1590	Hideyoshi victorious in subjugating all daimyo to his vassalage and commands supreme power in Japan.
1592	Hideyoshi leads expedition to Korean peninsula. Plans the occupation of Korea and Ming China.
1594	Execution of Christians in Nagasaki. Construction of Fushimi castle for Hideyoshi.
1597	Hideyoshi's second Korean expedition initiated.
1598	Hideyoshi dies and is succeeded by his son, Toyotomi Hideyori (1593–1615).
1600	Tokugawa Ieyasu (1542–1616) is victorious in the Battle of Sekigahara and emerges as rival to the Toyotomi cause.
1602	Construction of Ieyasu's Nijo castle.
1603	Ieyasu appointed shogun.
1610	Construction of Ieyasu's Nagoya castle.
1615	Ieyasu's seige of Osaka castle. Toyotomi clan defeated. Tokugawa shogunate establishes unchallenged rule that lasts until 1868.

GLOSSARY

bushi: Armed fighter or warrior; also called samurai.

daimyo: Feudal warlord; local military and administrative head of a domain.

eboshi: The traditional headgear worn by courtiers and high-ranking samurai.

fukigaeshi: Lateral backturned flaps of the Japanese helmet.

gindami: A decorative lacquer technique whereby silver dust is sprinkled over a coat of damp lacquer, allowed to dry, then applied with transparent lacquer, and finally polished. The resulting surface is a dull silver sheen.

harikake: A material composed of laminated paper or leather; often used to shape three-dimensional forms surmounting helmets. Several layers of the fibrous paper mulberry (*kōzo*) are pasted (*haru*) on wooden forms and allowed to dry. The wooden forms are then removed, in a process similar to papier-mâché. If made of leather, tanned skins are first soaked in water to soften, then they are pressed and hammered against wooden forms, and finally allowed to dry. The hollow shape in paper or leather is then finished with lacquer.

hōdan: Literally "cannonball." A term generally translated as "bullet-shaped" and used to describe an elongated form of helmet produced after the sixteenth century.

kabuto: Helmet. The term refers to the protective bowl (*hachi*) and to the neck-guard (*shikoro*).

kanasabi-ji: Rust surface. A metal surface produced by allowing the metal, usually iron in the case of helmets, to acquire its natural, rust-colored finish. A transparent coat of lacquer is often applied to protect the surface from over-rusting.

kawari kabuto: Literally "extraordinary" or "different helmet." The name given to a type of Japanese helmet that appeared in the sixteenth century and continued to be produced until the mid-nineteenth century. These helmets are so-called because they are different (*kawari*) from the standard helmet (*kabuto*). They are characterized by unique and individual three-dimensional forms attached to a protective helmet-bowl.

kinkarakawa: Tooled and gilded leather.

kuwagata: Literally "hoe-shaped." The most common decoration attached to traditional helmets, this U-shaped form is named after an agricultural hoe.

maedate: Frontal ornament adorning the helmet.

maki-e: A decorative lacquer technique whereby gold, silver, or copper dust is sprinkled in a pattern on damp clear lacquer. When the dust adheres and the lacquer is dry, excess powder is brushed away and the surface is polished.

namban: Literally "southern barbarian". This term refers to the Europeans who visited Japan, by a southern route, in the sixteenth and seventeenth centuries.

samurai: Armed fighter or warrior; also called *bushi*. From the twelfth through mid-nineteenth centuries, the samurai comprised the ruling military estate and were members of the highest social class.

Sengoku: Literally "country at war." The name given to the era of decentralized rule and civil war (1467–1573), characterized by the rise of the daimyo warlord.

Sengoku daimyo: Daimyo of the Sengoku era (1467–1573); the warlord class which rose to power in the late fifteenth and sixteenth centuries.

shikoro: Neck-guard of the traditional Japanese helmet.

shogun: Chief of the military estate. From the late twelfth through the mid-nineteenth centuries, the shogun was the *de facto* ruler of Japan.

takaki-nuri: Textured lacquer. Lacquer is mixed with fired, powdered earth, and painted thickly on the object being finished. Before it dries, it is lightly pounded (*tataku*) with a small ball of cloth-covered cotton to produce fine wrinkles in the surface. When dry, the lacquer has a textured, finely-corrugated surface.

tenugui: An oblong cloth, usually of cotton, traditionally used as a washcloth and often tied or placed on the head in various styles.

zukin: Hood. Traditionally made of cloth and worn over the head.

SELECTED BIBLIOGRAPHY

Anderson, L. J. *Japanese Armour.* London: Arms and Armour Press, 1968.

Berry, Mary Elizabeth. *Hideyoshi.* Cambridge: Harvard University Press, 1982.

Bolitho, Harold. *Treasures among Men: The Fudai Daimyo in Tokugawa Japan.* New Haven: Yale University Press, 1974.

Boxer, C.R. *The Christian Century in Japan 1549-1650.* Berkeley: University of California Press, 1951.

Compton, Walter A., Homma Junji, et al. *Nippon-Tō: Art Swords of Japan: The Walter A. Compton Collection.* New York: Japan Society, Inc., 1976.

Cooper, Micheal S.J., ed. *The Southern Barbarians.* Tokyo: Kodansha International Ltd., 1971.

——. *They Came to Japan: An Anthology of European Reports on Japan, 1543-1640.* Berkeley: University of California Press, 1965.

Dunn, Charles J. *Everyday Life in Traditional Japan.* Tokyo: Charles E. Tuttle Company, 1972.

Duus, Peter. *Feudalism in Japan.* New York: Alfred A. Knopf, 1969.

Elison, George and Bardwell L. Smith, eds. *Warlords, Artists, and Commoners: Japan in the Sixteenth Century.* Honolulu: University of Hawaii Press, 1965.

Hakuseki Arai. *The Armour Book in Honchō-Gunkikō*, translated by Otsuka Y., edited by H. Russell Robinson. Rutland, Vt: Charles E. Tuttle Company Inc., 1964.

Hall, John Whitney. *Japan: From Prehistory to Modern Times.* New York: Delacourte Press, 1970.

——, and Marius B. Jansen, eds. *Studies in the Institutional History of Early Modern Japan.* Princeton: University Press, 1968.

——, and Toyoda Tekeshi, eds. *Japan in the Muromachi Age.* Berkeley: University of California Press, 1977.

——, Nagahara Keiji and Yamamura Kozo, eds. *Japan Before Tokugawa: Political Consolidation and Economic Growth, 1500-1650.* Princeton: Princeton University Press, 1981.

Keene, Donald. *The Japanese Discovery of Europe: Honda Toshiaki and Other Discoveries, 1720-1798.* London: Routledge and Kegan Paul Ltd., 1952.

Lewis, Archibald. *Knights & Samurai: Feudalism in Northern France and Japan.* London: Temple Smith, 1974.

Nakano Masaaki, with introduction by Kaionji Chōgoro. *Katchū* (Armor). Tokyo: Nihon Tokyo Bujutsu, 1971.

Nickel, Helmut, Stuart W. Pyhrr, and Leonid Tarassuk. *The Art of Chivalry: European Arms and Armor from the Metropolitan Museum of Art.* New York: The Metropolitan Museum of Art and The American Federation of Arts, 1982.

Nitobe Inazo. *Bushido: The Soul of Japan.* Rutland, Vt: Charles E. Tuttle Co., 1969.

Noguchi, Isamu, with an introduction by R. Buckminster Fuller. *A Sculptor's World.* New York: Harper and Row, 1968.

Perrin, Noel. *Giving Up the Gun: Japan's Reversion to the Sword.* Boulder: Shambhala Publications, 1980.

Robinson, Russell H. *Introduction to Japanese Arms & Armor.* New York: Crown Publishers Inc., 1969.

Sakakibara Kōzan. *The Manufacture of Armour and Helmets in Sixteenth Century Japan (Chukokatchū Seisakuben)*, translated by T. Wakameda, revised and edited by H. Russell Robinson. Rutland, Vt: Charles E. Tuttle Company Inc., 1963.

Sansom, George. *A History of Japan 1615-1867*. Stanford: Stanford University Press, 1963.

——. *Japan: A Short Cultural History*. New York: Appleton-Century-Crofts, Inc., 1962.

The Taiheiki: A Chronicle of Medieval Japan. Translated with an introduction by Helen Craig McCullough. New York: Columbia University Press, 1959.

The Tale of the Heike. Translated by Kitagawa Hiroshi and Bruce T. Tsuchida, with a foreword by Edward Seidensticker. Tokyo: University of Tokyo Press. 1975.

Tani Shin'ichi and Sugase Tadashi. *Namban Art: A Loan Exhibition from Japanese Collections*. Washington D.C.: International Exhibitions Foundation, 1973.

Tokyo National Museum. *Nihon no Buki Bugu* (Japanese Arms and Armor). Tokyo: Tokyo National Museum, 1976.

Totman, Conrad D. *Politics in the Tokugawa Bakufu 1600-1843*. Cambridge: Harvard University Press, 1967.

——. *Tokugawa Ieyasu: Shogun*. San Francisco: Heian International Inc., 1983.

Tsuji Nobuo, Moriya Takeshi, and Suzuki Keizō, edited by Miyazaki Takashi. *Sengoku no Kawari Kabuto* (Spectacular Helmets of the Sengoku Era). Tokyo: Kadodawa Shoten, 1984.

Turnbull, S. R. *The Samurai: A Military History*. New York: Macmillan Company, 1977.

Varley, H. Paul. *Samurai*. New York: Delacourte Press, 1971.

定価8,500円
in Japan